PRAISE FOR
THE SOFT SKILLS BOOK

"This book is full of awesomeness. It has shedloads of very useful, simple frameworks to improve your thinking and decision making. I highly recommend it."

John Acton, Managing Partner at DPI

"This book is a great guide. It's visual, to the point, and full of ideas on how to approach things. I'd definitely recommend it for both personal and professional inspiration."

Gemma Butler, Marketing Director at The Chartered Institute of Marketing

"The ability to make the complex simple is a rare talent. Dan has done this previously in marketing and has now brought his brilliant drawings and writing to soft skills – those human fundamentals we all know are important but often neglect; how we live, communicate and work better."

Tim Sparke, Founder of Congregation.io

"I recommend this book to all my graduating seniors. Dan breaks down every critical soft skill that students need in order to succeed. Each principle is illustrated in Dan's unique style to make it easier to understand and apply. Every important soft skill is addressed – managing yourself, building teams, managing others, project management, effective presentations, etc. I wish I had this book when I was starting my marketing career."

Tom Elmer, Adjunct Professor of Marketing,
West Chester University of Pennsylvania

"Jam-packed with concise and valuable information – only the important stuff without the pretentious buzzwords. Genuine, honest and gutsy information that would be beneficial for any manager or person wanting to get to the next level in their career."

Angela Argyrou, Marketing Manager at Chempro Chemists

"Clear, straightforward and practical. Illuminated by the author's excellent diagrams."

James Hankins, Founder at Vizer Consulting

"Very accessible and digestible with lots of bite-size tips and guidance. An ideal aid for people to dip in and out of when the need arises."

Rebecca Wynberg, Founder and Head at Sadek Wynberg Research

"*The Soft Skills Book* is extremely useful, practical and very relevant for our business. I look forward to buying it for my team."

Dr. Maria Darma, Managing Director at Kantar Insights Belgium

FOR OTHER TITLES IN THE SERIES...

CONCISE ADVICE LAB

SMALL BOOKS: BIG IDEAS

CLEVER CONTENT, DYNAMIC IDEAS, PRACTICAL
SOLUTIONS AND ENGAGING VISUALS –
A CATALYST TO INSPIRE NEW WAYS OF THINKING
AND PROBLEM-SOLVING IN A COMPLEX WORLD

conciseadvicelab.com

Published by
LID Publishing Limited
The Record Hall, Studio 304,
16-16a Baldwins Gardens,
London EC1N 7RJ, UK

info@lidpublishing.com
www.lidpublishing.com

A member of:

BPR
businesspublishersroundtable.com

Inspiration and invaluable editorial advice generously provided by Alex White.

© Dan White, 2021
© LID Publishing Limited, 2021
Reprinted in 2021, 2022

Printed in Latvia by Jelgavas Tipogrāfija

ISBN: 978-1-911671-54-1
ISBN: 978-1-911671-55-8 (ebook)

Cover and page design: Caroline Li

THE
SOFT
SKILLS
BOOK

THE KEY DIFFERENCE TO BECOMING
HIGHLY EFFECTIVE AND VALUED

DAN WHITE

MADRID | MEXICO CITY | LONDON
NEW YORK | BUENOS AIRES
BOGOTA | SHANGHAI | NEW DELHI

CONTENTS

INTRODUCTION

In a world where automation is changing the face of business, employers are increasingly looking for skills that machines cannot replicate. They need people who can collaborate well, build strong relationships, manage projects effectively, and influence decision-makers within and outside the company.

The challenge is acquiring these 'soft skills.' Few companies have the resources to have staff take all the relevant training courses. If you are lucky, you'll learn from the people you work with by observing how they handle different situations and by asking lots of questions. However, not all bosses have the knowledge or inclination to provide reliable advice. This is where *The Soft Skills Book* comes in. It has been written for anyone keen to develop and apply their soft skills over the course of their career. The book has been structured to reflect the order in which you will probably need to develop different skills, although the exact sequence will vary a lot between different types of job. You can refer to *The Soft Skills Book* for advice and practical tips when facing a challenge for the first time or looking for inspiration to tackle a familiar predicament in a new way.

The first two chapters are about getting yourself organized, physically, mentally and practically — skills you'll need from the beginning of your working life. Chapters 3 and 4 are about managing, nurturing, and motivating individuals and teams. These are for when you are given people-management or leadership responsibilities for the first time. Chapter 5 is for when you're first put in charge of a project. It provides an overview of key processes and best practices, including lots of practical tools and templates. Chapter 6 is an introduction to developing your professional network – how to gain new contacts, make a good impression and keep in touch with people who might help you later on in your career. The final four chapters focus on sharing and co-creating ideas. Chapter 7 introduces the art of developing a clear, compelling story, and Chapter 8 describes how to deliver it with impact. Chapters 9 and 10 then provide more detail about the specific skills needed for leading successful workshops and delivering new business pitches.

Over a career spanning 30 years, the author of *The Soft Skills Book* has managed teams large and small, coached and mentored numerous business professionals, and led hundreds of presentations, workshops and pitches. This experience, combined with his passion and flair for training and development, led to him becoming Head of Expertise for the UK office of Kantar, a global data, insights and consulting company. In that capacity, he was responsible for enhancing the professional capabilities of the organization's executives. Throughout his career, the author researched each new skill he needed to acquire and drew sketches, notes and frameworks to capture what he learned and help share it with others. These illustrations have been collected together in *The Soft Skills Book*. Each illustration has been fleshed out with clear, concise explanations to guide you every step of the way.

The Soft Skills Book is an indispensable guide for anyone eager to develop professionally. Every job requires different strengths and capabilities, but soft skills form the backbone of any successful career.

PART ONE

THINGS YOU ARE OR
COULD BE GOOD AT

THINGS YOU FIND
REWARDING

THINGS THAT PAY
ENOUGH

YOU

1.1 PHYSICAL HEALTH

If you want to succeed in any walk of life, you'll need to look after your body. Life can present many challenges, but if you're physically healthy, you'll be able to cope much better with anything that happens and be more likely to achieve your goals.

If you already strive to keep your body in top condition, feel free to skip ahead to the next section. If, like the author, you prefer a Toblerone to a triathlon, consider how your lifestyle is affecting your potential. This section serves as a reminder that if you want to have a long, successful career, you'll need your body to last the distance. Even small adjustments to your daily routine can a make a big difference in the long run. So, if you've never thought much about your health, consider how you could make improvements in three key areas: diet, exercise and sleep. Here are some tips:

LOOKING AFTER YOUR BODY

DIET

Maximize variety
Minimize alcohol
Mind calories
Stay hydrated

EXERCISE

Make it habitual
Do what you enjoy
Build up gradually
Count daily steps

SLEEP

Have wind-down routine
No screens in bedroom
Count day's highlights
Try mindfulness app

DIET

A varied diet is a healthy diet. Your body needs nutrients that come from a wide variety of foods, so avoid choosing the same things every week. Eating fruit and vegetables that span the rainbow of colours is a great way to ensure that your body gets the range of nutrients it needs. Alcohol is a depressant, so it may help you relax at first, but as you drink more it tends to amplify any feelings of anxiety or depression. If you want to reduce your weight, controlling the calories you eat is by far the most effective strategy. All weight-loss diets involve taking in fewer calories than your body burns each day, so choosing certain foods can help you accomplish this. Depending on whom you talk to, the secret to weight loss is either eating a higher proportion of foods that increase your metabolism or filling yourself up on low-calorie foods. Some foods can do both of these, so they're a safe bet if you want to lose weight.

The evidence that some foods burn calories faster than others isn't strong. On the other hand, evidence that some foods are more filling relative to their calories is compelling.

FOODS FOR CONTROLLING YOUR WEIGHT

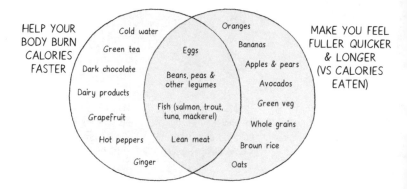

HELP YOUR
BODY BURN
CALORIES
FASTER

Cold water

Green tea

Dark chocolate

Dairy products

Grapefruit

Hot peppers

Ginger

Oranges

Eggs

Bananas

Apples & pears

Beans, peas &
other legumes

Avocados

Fish (salmon, trout,
tuna, mackerel)

Green veg

Whole grains

Lean meat

Brown rice

Oats

MAKE YOU FEEL
FULLER QUICKER
& LONGER
(VS CALORIES
EATEN)

EXERCISE

We all know that getting regular exercise is healthy, but there are plenty of us who simply don't enjoy it. If the thought of getting sweaty and out of breath isn't your idea of fun, you can motivate yourself to exercise regularly by:

- Reminding yourself of the benefits you'll enjoy when you're healthier
- Setting goals based on tiny increments — if you managed five minutes of exercise on Day One, aim for six minutes on Day Two
- Finding a friend who also wants to exercise more, so you can encourage each other to keep going
- Catching up with your favourite entertainment; exercising provides a great opportunity for listening to music and audio books or re-watching your favourite TV box sets

If energetic exercise really doesn't appeal to you, taking regular walks can have huge health benefits. Just taking a 45-minute walk each day (around 6,000 steps) will do you a world of good. This should make it easier for you to reach the recommended 10,000 steps — the equivalent of five miles — by the end of the day, especially if you avoid sitting at a desk or lying on a couch for too long.

SLEEP

Sleep is important because it refreshes you physically and mentally. If you're struggling to get a good night's sleep, there are many remedies worth trying — ask your doctor for advice. Sticking to a deliberate 'wind down' routine can help. This means avoiding watching screens for an hour or so before you want to go to sleep, and doing the same relaxing things each night so you start to associate the routine with going to sleep. Your routine could involve taking a bath, reading a book or reflecting on the five best things that happened to you during the day. These kinds of mindful activities are explored in more detail in the next section.

1.2 MENTAL HEALTH

In the past, mental health issues were stigmatized, but many business leaders now appreciate that they're fundamentally no different than physical ailments. They come and go, are often treatable with medicine or other therapies, and don't necessarily have any impact on our occupational abilities and potential. There are many excellent resources available for anyone struggling with mental health challenges. You will find advice on your public or private health organizations' websites or through mental health charities.

Before COVID-19 arrived, the World Health Organization described stress as "the global health epidemic of the 21st century," with work-related issues often cited as the primary cause. If you experience anxiety due to work, there are many ways to build your resilience and reduce its effects. Here are some of them:

- Take a ten-minute break every hour and a half to clear your head
- Allocate blocks of hours each week when you'll avoid working altogether
- Foster a growth mindset (see Section 1.4) to help you avoid dwelling on perceived failures

- Stay close to friends and family — the people you can rely on for emotional support when you need it
- Practise mindfulness

When you feel anxiety building up, you can use the mindfulness techniques summarized below to help calm yourself down. Just stop what you're doing and spend a few moments in a mental 'oasis.'

YOUR MENTAL OASIS

OBSERVE   ACCEPT   SENSE   IMAGINE   SYMPATHIZE

OBSERVE

A great way to take your mind away from what was making you anxious is to observe what's going on. Start by noticing what it feels like in your chest as you breathe in and out slowly, maybe four or five times. Observe what's going on around you (what you can see, hear, smell, etc.) and then reflect on what's happening inside your head. For instance, you may be thinking, 'I'm feeling anxious right now,' 'I keep thinking about X,' 'I think I'm worrying about X,' etc. Simply making yourself aware of these things will help you start to calm down.

ACCEPT

The next step is to accept that it's perfectly normal for people to become anxious from time to time. The complexities and pressures of the modern world are enough to create stress for anyone, but it's important to remember that feelings of anxiety always pass over time.

SENSE

If you spend a few minutes focusing on your senses, it helps alleviate stressful feelings. Try zeroing in on what you can feel in your toes, and then your legs, abdomen, arms, neck and head. This is a meditative technique known as a 'body scan.' It can take your mind away from what was troubling it and help you feel calm, relaxed and 'in the moment.'

IMAGINE

To achieve a deeper level of relaxation, try imagining yourself in a beautiful, tranquil place — an oasis where you can relax and be at peace for a while. Use your imagination to make this place as vivid and memorable as possible, adding details that make it feel special to you. This is your 'safe place,' which you can conjure up whenever you need to settle your mind, take a step back from the daily grind and remember what's important in life.

SYMPATHIZE

Stress and sadness are often the result of people being too hard on themselves. People sometimes say things about themselves in their head that they'd never say to their worst enemies, and these words can be extremely hurtful. Thankfully, they're rarely close to the truth. Try to be sympathetic to yourself in the same way you are to others. Nobody's perfect, so even if you haven't been at your best recently, try to forgive yourself, promise to try to do better in future and move on.

Everyone has times when they feel anxious, overwhelmed or down, and the mindfulness techniques described above can help cope with these moments. If you're struggling with unhelpful thought patterns because they recur frequently, your doctor can help you find a remedy. Even if you don't find a way to eradicate the issue completely, it's no big deal. A large portion of the population is in the same boat, the author included, and there's no reason you can't have an amazing, rewarding, successful life despite the ongoing challenge.

1.3 TIME MANAGEMENT

Time is a precious commodity. Successful people tend to make time for what's important to them by minimizing the time they spend on dull, unimportant things. If you want to advance your career, build personal relationships, relax and enjoy your personal life, you need to find ways to minimize time spent on low-value activities. Here are four things you can do to help:

WORKING EFFICIENTLY

PLAN YOUR TIME

SET TIME LIMITS

WORK IN BATCHES

SWAP WITH YOUR TEAM

PLAN YOUR TIME

This means deciding what to do and when. A good tip is to plan the week ahead in broad brushstrokes and the day ahead in detail. Schedule complex tasks for when you're at your best (early on, if you're a morning person) or when you know you won't be disturbed.

SET TIME LIMITS

For less important tasks, it's worth setting yourself a time limit. If you do, there's a good chance you'll complete the task on time. If you don't give yourself a deadline, you'll invariably work for longer than the task warrants.

WORK IN BATCHES

Most of us think we can multi-task, but it has been proven that everybody works better if they focus on one thing at a time. This is especially true for repetitive tasks because we get faster as we go along. It pays to do these in batches, like responding to emails in bulk. It's also helpful to avoid distractions, such as responding to messages, in order to maximize our concentration and minimize the time taken.

SWAP WITH YOUR TEAM

A great way of saving time is to swap work with colleagues, allowing you to focus on what you do best and can do quickly. Meanwhile, your colleagues focus on tasks that you find particularly time consuming.

When it comes to deciding what you should spend your time doing, the task prioritization matrix can help. This grid is based on the principle that if something is important, it deserves time being devoted to it, and if something's urgent, it needs to be done soon.

TASK PRIORITIZATION MATRIX

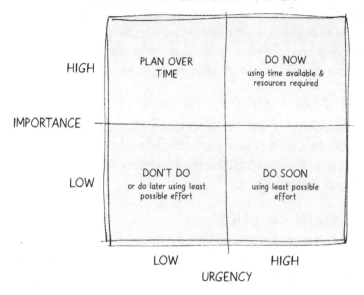

A lot of people find one simple piece of advice helpful: write things down. This has two huge benefits:

- You won't forget what needs to be done
- Your mind can relax, knowing that it doesn't have to keep a mental record of your 'To-Do List,' which creates a sense of calm that contributes to a good night's sleep

1.4 GROWTH MINDSET

Psychologist and Stanford University professor Carol Dweck high-lighted the value of a 'growth mindset' in her 2006 book, *Mindset: The New Psychology of Success*. It's a belief that people can develop new abilities over time. This contrasts with a 'fixed mindset,' which assumes that you're either good at something or not, and that no amount of practice will make much difference. The book highlights that people with a growth mindset:

- Have a less stressful and more successful life
- Learn faster and collaborate better
- Treat failure as a natural part of the learning process and don't allow it to undermine their self-worth
- Are more comfortable taking risks in order to achieve a goal

Here are some ways to foster a growth mindset in yourself and others:

FOSTERING A GROWTH MINDSET

BELIEVE IN POTENTIAL

SHOW BRAVERY

VALUE FEEDBACK

APPRECIATE FAILURE

APPLAUD EFFORT

CULTIVATE PATIENCE

BELIEVE IN POTENTIAL

Having a growth mindset means believing in people's capacity to continually develop and improve. Everyone has brain capacity to spare; a growth mindset means believing that anyone can use this capacity to become great at something if the conditions are favourable.

SHOW BRAVERY

We learn most from new experiences, so it pays to push ourselves out of our comfort zone into unfamiliar situations. For this to happen, we need the courage to raise our hand when opportunities arise, and leaders need to take calculated risks when deciding whom to assign to different challenges.

VALUE FEEDBACK

Feedback is vital for effective learning. When a golfer strikes the ball cleanly and it sails into the distance, they need to know what was right about their swing to help them do it again. When a business meeting turns into a train wreck, finding out why enables the next one to go more smoothly.

APPRECIATE FAILURE

Thomas Edison, the great American inventor, is believed to have said that he never failed – he just found thousands of ways that didn't work. Our attitude towards failure affects whether we'll take on new challenges and our resilience when things go wrong. Fear of failure holds us back; if we take on challenges knowing that a stumble will help us learn, we'll cope better with setbacks. Leaders need to create an environment that allows people to volunteer for tough challenges, safe in the knowledge that if they do their best, failure will not reflect badly on them.

APPLAUD EFFORT

To prevent failure being stigmatized, leaders should recognize and celebrate people's efforts regardless of success or failure. While this is rarely seen in a business context, placing as much value on effort and learning as on achievement would help create the right conditions for a growth mindset to flourish.

CULTIVATE PATIENCE

In his 2008 bestseller, *Outliers*, Canadian journalist Malcolm Gladwell showed how experts in any field have put in at least 10,000 hours of practice to master complex skills. He pointed out that Microsoft's Bill Gates spent thousands of hours programming the school computer, and the Beatles played more than 1,200 sets in the bars of Hamburg in the early 1960s before they became famous. Businesses and individuals need to acknowledge that learning takes time and that practice is required to achieve mastery.

1.5 CAREER CHOICES

People worldwide spend about a third of their life asleep, a third doing their own thing and a third at work. As the old adage goes, nobody has ever said on their deathbed that they wished they'd spent more time at the office. So, it's clear that people should try to pursue a career they find rewarding and enjoyable. If you're lucky enough to have multiple career opportunities, it's worth considering which to prioritize. Here is a simplified version of the excellent Japanese *Ikigai* ('reason for being') approach to finding career fulfilment and happiness:

CHOOSING YOUR CAREER

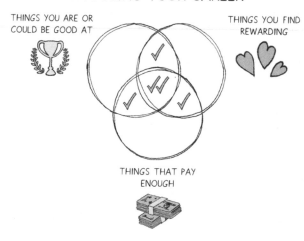

THINGS YOU ARE OR COULD BE GOOD AT

THINGS YOU FIND REWARDING

THINGS THAT PAY ENOUGH

The thinking is simple: your ideal career is one that combines the things you're good at and find rewarding, while delivering the level of income you need for the lifestyle you desire. Most people are lucky enough to find a job that fulfils one or two of these factors, so if you see an opportunity to achieve all three, by all means go for it!

The benefit of being happy and fulfilled at work is that you can focus all your remaining time and energy on your personal life, your happiness and the happiness of your loved ones.

In order to succeed in your chosen career, you'll need a growth mindset, determination and patience (and maybe a little luck now and again). Don't expect your career to progress in a linear fashion because good opportunities don't usually present themselves in a logical, timely way.

When an opportunity does arise, ask yourself whether you'll learn something that you'll need to be successful in your chosen career. If so, it could be an opportunity worth taking, even if at first glance it isn't the most obvious next step. Think of it as working your way up a climbing wall — a sideways move can often open up a better route to the top.

Whatever path you choose, even if it ends up very specialized, you'll go further if you continually develop your soft skills. These include how organized you are, how well you deal with other people, your leadership qualities and your ability to communicate effectively. All of these are covered in the chapters ahead.

PART TWO

PAY ATTENTION

PROBE

PAUSE

PLAY BACK

PRESENT POSSIBILITIES

OTHER PEOPLE

2.1 DIFFERENT PERSONALITIES

There are few walks of life that do not involve interacting with other people. Humans are social by nature, and much of our species' success has come from forming social bonds and collaborating for mutual benefit. This is as true today as it was 52 million years ago, when our ancestors discovered they were safer from predators if they formed groups.

To collaborate well with others, you need to understand that people differ immensely in what they find important and what motivates them. You'll need to modify what you say and do when dealing with different types of people if you want to influence them.

We're all aware that getting to know someone well can be fascinating, but it also helps you build strong relationships. Understanding what people care about allows you to connect with them personally and talk about things in a way they'll find relevant and interesting.

However, there will be occasions when you'll be dealing someone you haven't had a chance to get to know — for example, when pitching for new business. You may have to guess what their priorities and preferences are based on their behaviours. In these situations, it's helpful to consider people in terms of four basic personality types. Few people fit any one type perfectly, but it's a useful way of framing how you might want to approach them.

PERSONALITY TYPES

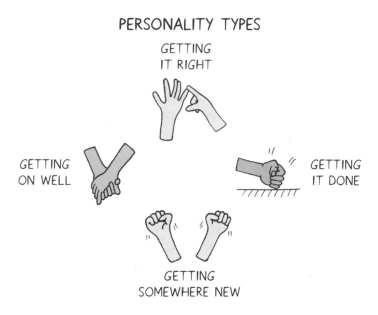

GETTING
IT RIGHT

GETTING
ON WELL

GETTING
IT DONE

GETTING
SOMEWHERE NEW

Here are some common characteristics of each type:

GETTING
IT RIGHT

- Measured and logical
- Precise and succinct
- Refers to facts and figures
- Quiet and less inclined to make small talk
- May be less tactile
- Uncomfortable with prolonged eye contact

GETTING
IT **DONE**

- Authoritative and formal
- Direct and to the point
- Tends to be impatient
- Socially confident
- Has a firm handshake
- Good at maintaining eye contact

GETTING
SOMEWHERE **NEW**

- Energetic and enthusiastic
- Creative and inspirational
- Keen to explore ideas
- Talkative and animated
- Tactile
- Smiles a lot

GETTING
ON **WELL**

- Welcoming and friendly
- Willing to explore emotions
- Invites social banter
- Brings people into conversations
- Tends to be more tactile
- Warm handshake

Although people don't fall neatly into these categories, being aware of how individuals differ can help you look out for these traits and adjust your style of interaction accordingly. The kinds of adjustments you can make are explored in the next section.

2.2 HANDLING DIFFERENT PERSONALITIES

We should always try to be our natural selves and avoid putting on an act just to impress or manipulate others. However, people differ in what they care about and respond to, and trying to accommodate these differences makes collaboration easier. It's also respectful and considerate. The ability to gauge people's preferences and accommodate them is especially important when dealing with those who are markedly different from you, such as people from distant cultures or another generation.

Section 2.1 described the behaviours that signal a particular personality type. This section explores what you can do to get along well with each type.

GETTING IT RIGHT

Someone who takes time to it GET IT RIGHT prides themself on their rigour and diligence. It pays to invite them to provide the checks and balances — for example, by reviewing a project's feasibility or estimating costs. They may be socially reserved, and if you sense that they are, respect their personal space and don't rush them into pressurized social situations.

GETTING IT DONE

If you identify someone itching to GET IT DONE, they probably prefer to be in charge. So, allow them to take the lead if it's appropriate to do so. If you share this trait with a superior, be careful not to antagonize them by competing for attention and control. People who express this trait like to get on with things and make decisions quickly, so be brief and to the point when dealing with them and keep the chit-chat to a minimum.

GETTING SOMEWHERE NEW

People who like to GET SOMEWHERE NEW tend to have lots of ideas they want to share and discuss, so let them take centre stage from time to time. Allow them to share their stream of thoughts out loud if they want to; this helps them express their ideas properly. Any promising ideas can be captured and vetted for further development.

GETTING ON WELL

People who want everyone to GET ON WELL are interested in understanding and catering to individuals' needs and desires, so give them the opportunity to express their caring side. To collaborate effectively, it's important to listen to them and establish where they're coming from so you can build a rapport.

The grid below illustrates how to develop strong relationships with people, depending on their personalities.

WORKING WELL WITH DIFFERENT PERSONALITIES

	GETTING IT DONE	GETTING IT RIGHT	GETTING SOMEWHERE NEW	GETTING ON WELL
PERSUADE VIA:	End results	Rationale	New experiences	Team success
REASSURE VIA:	Guarantees	Evidence	Imagination	Listening
PROVIDE:	Schedules	Details	Possibilities	Harmony
ENSURE MEETINGS ARE:	Focused	Structured	Fun	Discursive
ENSURE TIMELINES ARE:	Adhered to	Pre-defined	Flexible	Realistic
RESPECT THEIR:	Pride	Privacy	Self-expression	Feelings
ACKNOWLEDGE THEIR:	Achievements	Rigour	Ideas	Emotional intelligence
PROVIDE OPPORTUNITIES TO:	Take the lead	Deliberate	Take the stage	Share feelings
GIVE RESPONSIBILITY FOR:	Chairing	Accuracy	Innovation	Team development
SET OBJECTIVES THAT ARE:	Ambitious	Precise	Inspiring	People-orientated
DISCUSS THE PROSPECT OF:	Promotion	Accolade	Excitement	Relationships

2.3 LISTENING SKILLS

If you want to have a rewarding and successful career, the most valuable skill you could ever learn is how to listen effectively. Listening skills are also the key to developing strong, lasting relationships in your personal life. Your ability to listen to others and understand where they're coming from is an essential life skill. If you want to succeed in life, this is the most important section in this book. In fact, you'll see that listening skills are referred to in later sections more often than any other topic.

Being a great listener is valuable because:

YOU FIND OUT WHAT REALLY MATTERS TO PEOPLE. This means you're better positioned to offer relevant advice, make well-informed decisions and positively influence people's lives.

YOU HELP PEOPLE THINK THINGS THROUGH. When someone has a problem to solve, you can often help them identify a solution for themselves simply by listening to them and asking relevant questions. This is a truly magical benefit if you are their manager — especially if you don't have the answer yourself!

YOU BUILD STRONGER RELATIONSHIPS. When you listen to someone, you show them respect and consideration, and this builds trust and empathy. This is true at work and at home.

IT HELPS YOU REMEMBER THE CONVERSATION. By being attentive throughout, you will remember all the important content without having to try.

To become a great listener, you just need to keep practising the '5Ps' approach:

HOW TO LISTEN WELL – THE 5 Ps

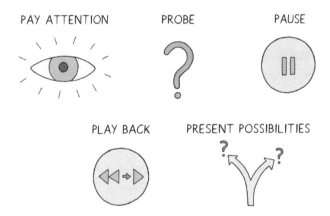

PAY ATTENTION

PROBE

PAUSE

PLAY BACK

PRESENT POSSIBILITIES

PAY ATTENTION to show your interest and create better engagement:
- Maintain eye contact and keep smiling
- Nod and make affirming, encouraging sounds
- Avoid interrupting
- Focus on what the other person is saying
- Imagine what they are feeling

PROBE to understand better by asking questions:

- 'Why do you say that?'
- 'Could you tell me more about that?'
- 'What are your thoughts on that?'
- 'Are you comfortable with X?'
- 'What do you need from X?'

PAUSE to allow the truth to come out:

- Don't fill silences
- Be patient — just wait for the other person to speak
- Some people need time before they're ready to express important things
- What people really feel may come out after a surprisingly long pause

PLAY BACK key points to show that you've been listening:

- Describe what you've understood about the person's situation
- Include their feelings as well as the facts
- Use your own words to demonstrate that you've genuinely understood
- Use phrases like, 'It sounds like what you're saying is X'

PRESENT POSSIBILITIES to identify solutions:

- Test the water by suggesting different scenarios
- Use questions like, 'Would X be an acceptable outcome for you?'
- Or, 'What if X were to happen, instead of Y?'
- Ask what might work for them
- Avoid being patronizing by telling the person what to do

2.4 PERSONAL MOTIVATIONS

If you've taken the time to get to know someone and used your listening skills to find out what's truly important to them, you'll probably understand what motivates them as well as they do themselves. This goes beyond the basic assessment of personality types covered in sections 2.1 and 2.2. It requires a deep understanding of what makes the person tick — what fundamentally influences their decisions and actions.

The following diagram shows many of the different motivational drivers a person might have. The four in the middle are common to almost everyone, but individuals differ in terms of which of the motivations in the outer circle they find most compelling. It's worth spending a minute or so to see if you can identify the areas that resonate most powerfully with you. If you want to form a strong, long lasting professional relationship with someone, you'll need to find out which of these dimensions they cherish highly.

PERSONAL MOTIVATIONS

Only by talking to people, being curious about what's important to them and listening well will you be able to discover their true motivations. If you can establish what people genuinely care about, you'll be in a much better position to work with them and help them achieve their goals. If you believe you can help them, make sure they know that you can, and then do your best to make it happen. The strongest relationships are two-way, so if someone offers to help you achieve what you want, and you accept their generosity, you'll both feel good and the relationship will become stronger.

2.5 HANDLING CONFLICT

Conflict in business life is as inevitable as it is within families — it's baked into our human DNA. So, it's important that you know how to cope with it when it inevitably rears its ugly head. Handling conflict well not only diffuses the immediate tension but can also lead to a trusting, long-term partnership. The most important thing to remember is that when someone's angry, they need someone else to acknowledge their anger and hear about what has upset them. Once this understanding has been established, the solution is often surprisingly easy to find.

Regardless of how the conflict came about, there is an approach that has been proven to help alleviate the situation every time. It requires you to be 'ALERT' to any potential problems. If you detect an issue early, you have an opportunity to address it before it grows into a festering ball of anger and frustration. The following framework is designed to help you handle any confrontational situation effectively:

HANDLING CONFLICT

ACKNOWLEDGE   LISTEN   EXPLORE   RATIFY   THANK

ACKNOWLEDGE

The first step it to acknowledge that the person you're dealing with is unhappy. It helps to say something like, 'I can see that you're unhappy about the situation.' Showing that you empathize with the disgruntled person goes a long way towards calming them down.

LISTEN

If you listen well (see Section 2.3) to understand the issue in detail, it makes the person realize that you genuinely want to help resolve the situation.

EXPLORE

Try exploring potential solutions by asking questions such as, 'What would help most?' And test options by asking, 'How about if...?'

RATIFY

If you reach a mutually acceptable agreement, take time to describe it clearly, confirm your commitment to it and check whether the other party is happy with it.

THANK

At the end of the discussion, thank the person for taking the trouble to highlight the issue and for spending time with you to resolve it.

The process outlined above has been proven to be highly effective. What's important is that the person appreciates that their point of view has been heard and that you've done something to make amends based on what they've said. Handling conflict well requires all the skills described earlier in Chapter 2: listening to the person to understand their anger, judging how to handle the situation based on their personality and establishing what they're seeking to achieve.

PART THREE

RELEVANT TO
CAREER AMBITIONS

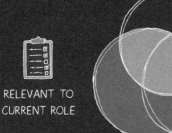

RELEVANT TO
CURRENT ROLE

RELEVANT TO OTHER
ROLES IN COMPANY

MANAGERS

3.1 MANAGERIAL APPROACH

There is no specific personality type or approach that makes someone a good manager. Effective management depends on being clear about what you need from your employees and doing your best to get the most from each of them. Listening to your team, treating each individual with respect and having a genuine desire to help them develop their knowledge and skills will go a long way towards achieving this. Great managers nurture the abilities of their employees and inspire them to pursue a career path they'll find rewarding (see Section 1.5).

The right approach to take when managing someone depends on:
- The team's overall objectives or immediate priorities
- The experience and capabilities of the individual
- The personalities, potential, motivations and ambitions of other team members

Accounting for these varied considerations makes management a major challenge. The framework below helps managers identify the approach best suited to their current circumstances. It shows that when the stakes are high and time is short, managers should be more prescriptive. This is particularly important with an employee lacking experience. You can give greater freedom and more opportunities for learning when the risks are low and time allows.

CHOOSING THE RIGHT MANAGERIAL APPROACH

	LOW RISK	DAY TO DAY	CRISIS
INEXPERIENCED INDIVIDUAL	COACHING	PARTICIPATIVE	DIRECTIVE
EXPERIENCED INDIVIDUAL	FREE REIN	VISIONARY	PARTICIPATIVE

Inexperienced individuals tend to learn quickly if they're given responsibilities for low-risk projects and only provided with guidance when it's asked for or absolutely essential.

COACHING

When an inexperienced employee is working in a low-risk scenario, you can give them something to own and just enough advice to ensure that they learn from the experience. This builds their confidence, gives them a sense of achievement and helps them become more resourceful, decisive and independent. As manager, your role is to then keep a close eye on progress and only provide guidance if you see things going awry.

PARTICIPATIVE

This approach is a great default for day-to-day management. You define the objectives but ask for employees' input to co-create the plan. You only use your first-among-equals status when needed to resolve a conflict or finalize a decision. A participative approach involves actively checking, on a daily basis, what team members are doing and providing your input if and when it is helpful.

DIRECTIVE

When you need employees to act without debate or delay, you will need to tell them exactly what to do. In a well-run business, this style of management is rarely required. However, in the event of a crisis, the business's reputation — and survival — is more important than the individual's development. So, inexperienced team members may need to be given explicit instructions and firm managerial oversight.

Experienced teams, on the other hand, should be given more freedom.

FREE REIN

When business is running smoothly, an experienced team member can be given licence to do whatever they think is best for the business, especially if the financial or reputational risk of failure is low. They can be given the freedom and resources to stretch out and experiment as they see fit. This can lead to breakthrough thinking and create new opportunities for the business.

VISIONARY

In day-to-day business matters, an experienced individual can be given authority to make their own decisions, based on the company's culture and vision. As manager, your job is to continually remind your people of the end goal and motivate them to figure out the best way of getting there.

PARTICIPATIVE

In a crisis scenario, managers with experienced team members should adopt a consultative approach, drawing on their collective experience and intelligence to identify the best route forward.

3.2 DELEGATING

Businesses with a hierarchical structure need to delegate effectively in order to keep costs down and deliver value to customers. Tasks should generally be assigned to the lowest-paid person capable of performing them. This requires effective delegation: junior team members being briefed on important tasks and empowered to perform them without significant senior intervention. The 'POUCH' framework illustrates the principles of effective delegation:

DELEGATING EFFECTIVELY

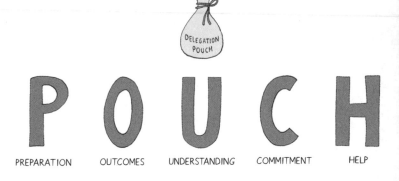

P	O	U	C	H
PREPARATION	OUTCOMES	UNDERSTANDING	COMMITMENT	HELP

The 'POUCH' represents the high stakes associated with delegation and the importance of trust. Successful delegation means finding someone you can rely on to do the job and trusting them to get on with it once you've briefed them.

PREPARATION

This involves identifying who is able to complete the task and briefing them thoroughly. To guarantee success, the designated individual needs to have the knowledge, skills and resources necessary to complete the task well.

OUTCOMES

The person to whom you've delegated must understand what needs to be achieved, in what timeframe, and be aware of any other constraints related to the project. However, they should not be told exactly how to complete the task. Instead, they should be given the freedom to achieve the outcome in their own way.

UNDERSTANDING

When delegating a task to someone, it's important to ask them to play back the requirements in their own words. This provides an opportunity to point out missing details and for clarification if necessary.

COMMITMENT

Effective delegation requires the employee to guarantee on-time delivery. If they have any concerns about completing the task, ask what could prevent them from delivering successfully, discuss what would need to happen in order for them to pull it off and figure out how to make this happen.

HELP

Before leaving your employee to get on with the task, ask them to anticipate obstacles that might push them off track. For each potential obstacle, agree on the support they'll be given to overcome it.

Delegation is an important skill, but even if you've mastered it, you should still keep in regular touch with your employees to give them an opportunity to discuss topics that aren't related to specific tasks or projects. The best way to do this is via regular one-to-one conversations — perhaps 30–60 minutes each week, depending on their level of autonomy. These routine discussions build trust and provide an opportunity for the employee to broach personal or sensitive matters without the having to request a special meeting. One-to-ones are primarily for the team member's benefit, designed for them to ask questions, discuss ideas, request feedback and coaching, or raise concerns.

WEEKLY ONE-TO-ONES

EMPLOYEE

ASK FOR ADVICE/SUPPORT IF REQUIRED
ASK FOR FEEDBACK ON RECENT WORK
RAISE ANY CONCERNS

OFFER ADVICE/SUPPORT IF ASKED
PRAISE & FEEDBACK ON RECENT WORK
NEWS AFFECTING THEM (NOT THE WHOLE TEAM)

MANAGER

One-to-ones tend to work best if the employee talks through their progress and is encouraged to mention anything else they wish to discuss. The manager should listen actively and develop the conversation around whatever the person wants to talk about, providing feedback if requested but not using these catch-ups to appraise performance. If appropriate, the meeting could also be used to share progress updates, discuss upcoming work or flag changes in the business if these haven't already been covered in wider team meetings.

If the team works remotely for much or all of the time, the manager needs to check in with employees more often so they don't begin to feel isolated or demotivated. Talk with your people and find out what works best for each of them. Many who work remotely will find it helpful to have a quick catch-up at the same time each day, ideally using a video platform, so they can provide a progress report and highlight any emerging barriers or concerns.

3.3 GIVING FEEDBACK

Everyone benefits from feedback, but few people find it easy to give or receive. To get the most from feedback, it helps to think of it as a gift. Offer it to someone if you think they'll find it useful and receive it gracefully, knowing that it's been given with the best intentions. However, be aware that some gifts are entirely useless! Ideally, feedback should be given soon after whatever gave rise to it. When providing these observations, remember that you're delivering 'NEWS' to someone, and they may or may not be receptive to it. Use the approach below to help stay objective and ensure that the feedback's seen as constructive.

GIVING FEEDBACK

| NOTICE | EFFECT | WAIT | SUGGEST |

NOTICE

Describe what you observed them doing or saying. Don't make any assumptions about their underlying thoughts or motives and avoid being judgmental. Just stick to the facts. Report that 'You described her idea as naïve and laughable' rather than speculating that 'You tried to make a fool of her because she irritated you.'

EFFECT

Explain the impact you know, or believe, this had on the people who actually heard it or were told about it. For example, 'She looked at her feet after that, so I believe she was upset.'

WAIT

At this point, give the person time to take in what you've said and a chance to reflect. They will usually say something, and if so, listen to them actively (see Section 2.3).

SUGGEST

Finally, ask what they might do should a similar situation arise in future. If you agree with their ideas, tell them so. If you have additional thoughts, share them.

The 'NEWS' approach is ideal for everyday feedback, but there will be occasions when a manager needs to address more important issues. The approach described below works well for serious matters because it encourages an open, adult-to-adult discussion.

HANDLING IMPORTANT CONVERSATIONS

TOPIC

REASON

THEIR POV

YOUR BUILDS

ACTIONS

TOPIC

Explain briefly what you want to talk about, including the facts of the situation. For example, you might need to explain that the team has been asked to achieve cost savings.

REASON

Explain why the topic has to be discussed — for example, the team needs to work up a cost-cutting proposal and present it to senior management by the end of the week. At this stage, it's best not to tell the person specifically what needs to be done, even if you already have a clear idea.

THEIR POINT OF VIEW

Ask them for their take on the situation and listen actively to understand their point of view. Let them think through the consequences and share their thoughts on potential solutions. They might suggest, for example, that the company's advertising expenditure be reduced by 30% for the remainder of the year.

YOUR BUILDS

If their conclusions are the same as or better than yours, tell them. If not, state your point of view and explain it in the context of what they've already said. For example, demonstrate that the ad spend through year-end needs to be cut by 50% rather than 30%.

ACTIONS

To avoid any misunderstandings later, all parties should confirm at the end of the meeting what they've agreed to and clarify their follow-up actions.

3.4 COACHING

Coaching is possibly the most helpful and effective way for a manager to support an employee. The essence of coaching is helping someone to think through for themselves how to approach a task or tackle a problem. The 'GROW' model, first published in 1992 by Sir John Whitmore, a pioneer of the executive coaching industry, lays out a simple yet highly effective approach. It can be used to help your employee with any issue they are facing, even if you know nothing about the subject.

GIVING FEEDBACK

GOAL	REALITY	OPTIONS	WILL DO
What is the person's goal?	What is the current reality? How far is the goal?	What could they do to progress towards the goal?	What will they do to move towards the goal?

Here's an example of 'GROW' in action:

GOAL

Imagine a scenario in which a manager, Anita, wants her team to attend an expensive training course. Anita's boss helps her identify how to achieve her goal: submit a business case to the CFO before the budget is finalized.

REALITY

The reality is that Anita hasn't written a business case before. She assumes it should explain why the training is necessary, and document the cost, but doesn't know what else to include or how to make it persuasive.

OPTIONS

Anita considers asking a colleague, Hendrik, to write it. She could read up on business cases instead (her manager mentions an excellent website that provides helpful examples), or she could ask a board member what's expected. As she talks through the options, Anita identifies the pros and cons.

WILL DO

Anita rules out asking Hendrik (he's way too busy) or consulting a board member (the board is away all week), but she's happy to write it herself now that she knows about the website. So, she chooses that option.

'GROW' works because it helps people step back and think things through logically. Simply clarifying the goal can make the challenge a lot clearer, and when it comes to exploring options, the best solution becomes clear remarkably quickly.

As a manager, you're responsible for helping your employees pursue their career aspirations and gain relevant experience. To succeed in their chosen path, the person must be confident in their own potential, find ways to develop their capabilities and know how to identify good career opportunities. If you can support them in the areas below, you'll not only help their career, you'll also gain their trust and loyalty.

EMPOWERING PEOPLE TO FLOURISH

BUILD CONFIDENCE

OFFER CHALLENGE

PROVIDE INSPIRATION

REMOVE OBSTACLES

GIVE FEEDBACK

DISCUSS CAREERS

BUILD CONFIDENCE

You can build someone's confidence by trusting them with responsibility, praising them when they do a good job and telling them that you believe in their potential.

OFFER CHALLENGE

The best way to help someone develop quickly is to give them tasks that stretch them and allow them to acquire new knowledge and skills. Ideally, your employee should spend half their time in their comfort zone and the other half just outside it.

PROVIDE INSPIRATION

You can help someone build their capabilities by identifying an interest of theirs that could be expanded upon. Sharing related ideas and recommending further reading or experiences can fire their passion for the topic.

REMOVE OBSTACLES

People sometimes need help overcoming obstacles to their career progression. For example, your employee's prospects may be hampered by the prejudices of other managers. As a manager, you should seek to counter these through advocacy or ethical argument. Other obstacles, such as personal limitations, are best addressed via coaching or encouragement.

GIVE FEEDBACK

Feedback is a valuable gift (see Section 3.3). The most powerful feedback you can give comes from observing someone doing something right and celebrating it in public.

DISCUSS CAREERS

To help someone flourish in their career, you need to look out for opportunities within the team, or elsewhere within the organization, that would help them develop and progress faster than they might in their current position. If this means they leave your team, at least you'll know you helped do what's right for them.

3.5 PERSONAL OBJECTIVES

Great managers devise objectives that their employees see as fair and motivating. This requires balancing the needs of the individual with the priorities of the business. Whenever possible, objectives should be co-created using the framework below to ensure that they're mutually beneficial.

IDENTIFYING BALANCED OBJECTIVES

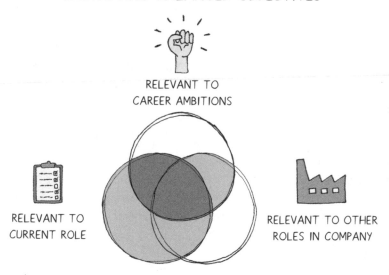

RELEVANT TO
CAREER AMBITIONS

RELEVANT TO
CURRENT ROLE

RELEVANT TO OTHER
ROLES IN COMPANY

Objectives need to relate to the person's current role, but the best ones also reflect the longer-term ambitions of the individual — this explains the darkest shading in the framework above. If someone hopes to move into a more senior role, one of their objectives could be tailored to help them develop the skills necessary for promotion.

It's good practice to set no more than four or five objectives, including one hard commercial outcome and one related to the individual's personal development. The popular 'SMART' framework can be used to ensure that all objectives are well thought through.

SETTING OBJECTIVES

SPECIFIC   MEASURABLE   ACHIEVABLE   RELEVANT   TIME-BOUND

SPECIFIC
Articulate what the outcome should be, why the objective has been set and how it will be achieved.

MEASURABLE
Clarify how performance in relation to the objective will be assessed.

Specify a number, percentage or value, or define how feedback will be obtained.

ACHIEVABLE

To be motivating, objectives should be challenging but realistic, given the resources available. According to productivity guru David Allen, objectives should be "51% achievable" — highly challenging yet just about attainable. Tough but achievable targets fire people's competitive instincts.

RELEVANT

Objectives need to relate to the unit's or whole company's targets, and to the person's individual responsibilities.

TIME-BOUND

Specify the timeline for completing the objective and, whenever possible, key milestones along the way so progress can be reviewed at appropriate times.

Objectives are typically set annually, and incremental progress towards them reviewed regularly. At the end of the year, the manager and employee usually meet to appraise how well the objectives have been met and to set fresh objectives for the year ahead. Appraisals should be conducted in a relaxed, informal, unhurried atmosphere. Set aside 60–90 minutes for the meeting and chose somewhere suitable for a private conversation. Most companies will have a formally prescribed process for annual employee appraisals, carefully vetted from an HR and business strategy standpoint. The conversation is generally managed along these lines:

BEFORE MEETING

- Employee and manager each assesses achievement versus objectives
- As part of this, manager collects data, evidence, feedback from others and specific examples to form a point of view
- Manager considers what next year's objectives might look like

DURING MEETING

- Employee shares their assessments
- Manager highlights any differences of opinion, and then listens (see Section 2.3)
- Manager refers to data, evidence, feedback and examples as necessary
- Employee talks about longer-term career aspirations
- Both discuss new knowledge and skills required, and ways they could be developed
- Manager shares thoughts on following year's objectives, adapted per the discussion
- Both discuss and agree on objectives and accompanying learning plan

AFTER MEETING

- Manager writes up what was agreed to, making objectives SMART(er) if necessary
- Employee checks the write-up, adds their comments if desired, and signs a document acknowledging the performance appraisal and forward-looking objectives

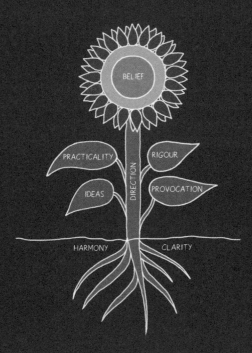

PART FOUR

TEAMS

4.1 TEAM CHARTER

In the best teams, people are happy, motivated and productive. Businesses rely on great teamwork, so if you've been put in charge of a team, you need to know how to make it successful.

A team leader's first task is to make sure every member knows what the group is trying to achieve and is genuinely on board. This is where a team charter comes in. It describes why the team exists, who's responsible for what, how the team operates and how its members are expected to behave. Your roles and rules help you achieve your goals; the organization's culture and values help people accept the rules and, where beneficial, remain flexible in terms of roles.

THE EFFECTIVE TEAM DIAMOND

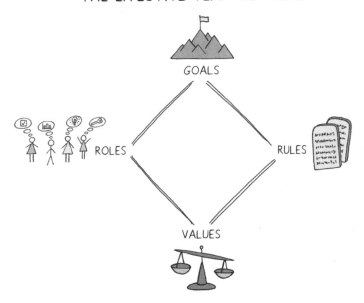

GOALS

These include the reason the team exists (often referred to as its mission) as well as more specific, short-term objectives. Having a set of clearly defined objectives creates a sense of purpose that helps motivate the team. It also helps team members understand and accept decisions made by the team leader, provided they relate to the team's goals.

ROLES

To work efficiently and harmoniously, each team member needs to be clear on their own areas of responsibility and how they're expected to work with the rest of the team. The team leader should take time to identity members' strengths, weaknesses and strongest motivations (see Sections 2.1 to 2.4). They can use this under-standing to establish roles that allow everyone to make a strong contribution and find their job rewarding. Team composition will influence how achievable this is. The ideal team consists of members whose skills cover what needs to be done, complementing one another neatly, with just enough overlap to accommodate absences.

RULES

These are the processes that all team members need to follow and behaviors that are deemed acceptable within the team. Rules typi-cally cover how team members are expected to communicate with each other, make decisions, resolve conflicts and handle excep-tional circumstances that might arise. New team members are required to confirm that they accept the rules when they join so that everyone feels empowered to flag any rule breaking, should it occur.

VALUES

Values are broader principles that team members are expected to uphold, which go beyond specific rules. Having a shared set of val-ues helps unite a team and create a mutually supportive, rewarding working environment.

Team values might include the following expectations of team members:
- To strive to do the best job they can
- To contribute to the team achieving its goals
- To identify opportunities for the team to become more effective
- To work the hours required to perform their duties, and speak up when hours are becoming excessive
- To be open and honest, while being respectful of people's feelings

- To be courteous and friendly to others
- To contribute to an inclusive environment in which everyone can express their thoughts and feelings
- To support fellow team members if they are under time or emotional pressure

Team values can be used to guide the selection of new team members and be referred to if a current member isn't contributing as they should.

When someone new joins the team, the leader should take time to explain the team charter and why it's important. This is especially important for teams that work remotely, as it can help the new recruit to start feeling part of something that goes beyond transactional relationships and equips them to collaborate well with other team members.

4.2 TEAM ROLES

Even the most impressive, well-rounded individuals are not good at everything. As a team leader, you need to recognize your own strengths and limitations and have the confidence to assemble a group of individuals who complement you. Great teams include people with different perspectives and a variety of strengths. An ideal team includes people who, between them, can fulfil all the roles illustrated below.

TEAM ROLES

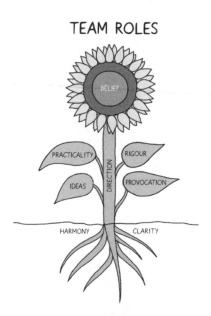

DIRECTION AND BELIEF

Teams need a leader to define what the group is out to achieve, or at least a chairperson who provides structure, drawing members' ambitions together to marshal the team's goals. Having clear goals helps the team stays focused, but success also depends on people being motivated to achieve them. This means that every team needs at least one person who instills belief and inspires the others – someone who makes the team blossom. This could be the leader or another charismatic team member who others look up to. People with the 'Get Somewhere New' tendency (see Section 2.1) are often good at this.

IDEAS AND PROVOCATION

To achieve its objectives, a team needs at least one or two people who can think creatively to help move the thinking on and come up with potential ways of solving problems. They provide the team with intellectual nourishment. To flourish, most teams benefit from having someone who considers the wider context and uses this to challenge the group's thinking and assumptions. They also won't shy away from standing up to the leader when they feel it's necessary.

RIGOUR AND PRACTICALITY

To avoid risking failure, teams also need someone able to weigh up the pros and cons of major decisions in an objective way. This person's role is to make sure all potential consequences are taken into consideration before the team finalizes a decision. People with the 'Get It Right' tendency are usually best suited to this role. Once a decision has been made, the team needs someone with the practical skills necessary to develop a workable plan and keep track of progress, to ensure that costs and schedules are adhered to.

HARMONY AND CLARITY

Even a team that has clear goals and effective plans is likely to fail if it isn't stable. At the root of any strong team is a harmonious way of working. Other team members may be able to provide direction and ambition that help unite the group, but it's often helpful to have one individual who fosters a collaborative team spirit. People with the 'Get on Well' tendency are ideal for this role. They may also play a role in ensuring that everyone remains grounded — clear about what the team has to achieve and how everyone needs to work together.

As team leader, it's your job to build a team that's able to fulfill all these roles, even if some members need to wear multiple hats.

4.3 TEAM MEETINGS

Teams of more than ten to 20 people sometimes struggle to feel like a true, cohesive unit, especially if some members rarely work with each other. Having an all-team meeting that lasts about an hour every month or so can help create a sense of team unity.

A well-planned and efficiently run team meeting can:
- Remind everyone to stay focused on the team's objectives
- Build team spirit and motivation
- Encourage collaborative work
- Address challenges requiring multiple perspectives

Effective team meetings typically include:

PROGRESS UPDATES

Each meeting should include a summary of the team's progress against objectives. This reminds everyone what the objectives are and encourages the team to stay focused on them. The progress update is also an opportunity to explain any implications of over- or under-performance, and any shifts in focus required during the remainder of the year.

FUN

It's worth setting aside ten minutes or so for an exercise unrelated to work that involves team members cooperating with one another. These short sessions can be highly entertaining and help people get to know each other. Look online for icebreakers or team building activities and choose whichever suit your organization's style, work well in a remote meeting if necessary and will take the amount of time you want to devote to this activity.

DISCUSSION

This segment is an opportunity for everyone to talk about a topic that's affecting, or could affect, the whole team's performance. The topic would ideally be relevant to the whole team and benefits from that fact that everyone is present to make a contribution. To help make these sessions constructive and inspiring, they should be positioned as opportunities to generate ideas and problem-solve rather than restating known difficulties.

CELEBRATION

Team meetings are a good opportunity for the team leader to thank everyone for their efforts and congratulate the group or individuals for recent accomplishments. Some teams also encourage members to give recognition to colleagues who've gone above and beyond in some way. Schemes of this sort can be themed around the team's values (if they've been identified), so that the organizational culture is reinforced at every meeting.

The graphic below captures a tried and trusted success formula for team meetings that you might find useful. To foster a sense of shared responsibility and collaboration, different combinations of members can be invited to run each team meeting, with introductory and closing words delivered by the team leader.

TEAM MEETING STRUCTURE

 Welcome everyone & share agenda

Fun team bonding activity

Summarize progress vs targets

Recognize & celebrate recent team & individual achievements

Share news affecting team objectives or ways of working

Workshop a topic related to team objectives/challenges

Thank everyone & end on optimistic high

Team meetings are key to building team spirit and a sense of collaboration, so they're particularly important for teams working remotely that sometimes struggle in this area.

4.4 COLLABORATING

The principles of business collaboration are the same regardless of whether the partnership is between different teams within the same organization or teams from different companies. Success always depends on identifying a 'win-win' — an arrangement that ultimately benefits both parties. It's worth being flexible and creative to find a solution that works for everyone, but don't be afraid to call time and avoid wasting further effort pursuing a fruitless opportunity.

EFFECTIVE COLLABORATION

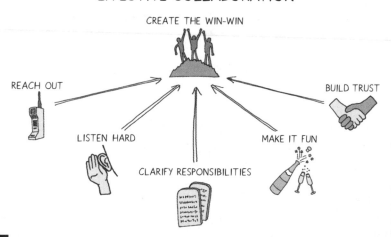

CREATE THE WIN-WIN

REACH OUT

BUILD TRUST

LISTEN HARD

MAKE IT FUN

CLARIFY RESPONSIBILITIES

REACH OUT

As a team leader, it is your responsibility to look for collaborative opportunities that would make your team more successful. If you come across such an opportunity, you should approach your potential partner to discuss what might be possible. See Section 6.2 for suggestions on how to make your approach.

LISTEN HARD

Potential partners will all have their own business priorities and may have reservations about collaborating with you. So, you need to ask lots of questions and listen well (see Section 2.3) to tease out any issues before you can identify a 'win-win.'

CLARIFY RESPONSIBILITIES

Once it's clear that a partnership is worthwhile, take the time to agree on who would be responsible for what and how the parties involved would keep in touch, interact and make decisions. Define these details before signing the deal to avoid frustration and wasted time later.

MAKE IT FUN

People love working with people they can relax and have fun with. So, if you want a collaboration to last, make an effort to create an enjoyable working relationship. Take the time to understand what makes your partners tick, and tailor your approach to them to show that their partnership is important to you.

BUILD TRUST

As with any relationship, a business collaboration is built on trust. Be open and honest with your partners and treat them with fairness, respect and courtesy (see Section 6.3). This is important from an ethical point of view, and will help bolster your reputation and engender loyalty from your business associates.

4.5 RECRUITING

How you bring in new members can have a big impact on your team's future success. Filling a vacancy with someone who is sub-standard or disruptive will impede productivity, impact morale and make the team less appealing for others to join. Recruiting the right person increases the team's breadth of perspectives and abilities, and makes being a member of the group more rewarding.

The starting point of the recruitment process is to write a job description. Below is an example that illustrates the types of information you'd normally want to include.

JOB DESCRIPTION

JOB TITLE	Marketing Director
REPORTING	Reports to Chief Marketing Officer
PURPOSE	Create interest in our offer and generate new business leads
HOURS	37.5 hours per week
LOCATION	Flexible mixture of working from home and in Manchester office
TRAVEL	London about once per week; occasional overnight trips abroad
RESPONSIBILITIES	Work with CMO to develop marketing strategy and detailed plans
	Develop and deliver a range of marketing materials and activities
	Manage relationships with external contractors
	Manage a team of 8 marketing executives
	Ensure costs stay within budget
QUALIFICATIONS	Marketing degree 2.1 or higher; MBA preferred
PROFICIENCIES	Competent in Adobe Photoshop and InDesign
EXPERIENCE	Managed a team of 4 or more for at least 3 years
	Been resposible for marketing budget of £150+
ABILITIES	Strong client handling responsibilities; can think on their feet; excellent project management; good attention to detail
BEHAVIOURS	Patient, collaborative, supportive, responsible
SALARY	Starting between £XX,XXX and £ZZ,ZZZ depending on experience

The job description provides candidates with an overview of what the role entails and allows them to determine whether they qualify. It's best to describe the job accurately, rather than trying to dress it up. This discourages unsuitable applicants and avoids promising something the job cannot deliver. The job description will also guide you (or HR) on where to advertise the role and help shape the selection process to identify the best applicants.

ADVERTISING THE POSITION

You should advertise the job in a way that reaches a diverse cross-section of relevant candidates. Avoid letting your own perspective affect where you chose to advertise. HR professionals can advise you on best practices, and there are plenty of articles online offering useful guidance on how to avoid unconscious bias.

SELECTION PROCESS

The right process depends on timing and budget, as well as the job requirements. The process should be guided by whichever elements of the job description are vital for success in the role. Selection methods should account for the following considerations:

- Aptitude tests are ideal for rejecting applicants who fall below a pre-defined minimum threshold in areas such as numeracy, literacy or technical understanding. Such tests, administered online, are commonly used as part of the initial screening process.
- Interviews are widely used and offer an effective way to identify strong candidates. They're ideal for understanding how someone approaches a challenge, their ability to think on their feet and whether what they've written in their application holds up under scrutiny. One of the most effective interview questions is: 'Please give me an example of when you X.'

- Although time consuming and expensive, group exercises are a good way to assess a candidate's teamworking and collaborative problem-solving capabilities. So, it makes sense to include them in the process if these abilities are crucial to the role. If the full selection process is conducted remotely, teamworking skills can be observed by talking to candidates as a group, using a video platform.
- Before confirming a job offer, it is good practice to contact at least two professional references the candidate has provided to confirm their experience and credentials and ask about their suitability for the role.

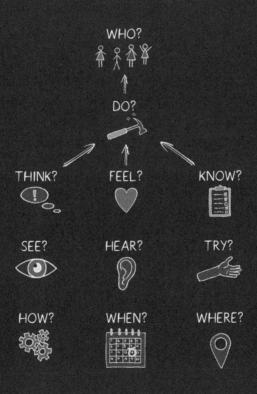

PART FIVE

WHO?

DO?

THINK?   FEEL?   KNOW?

SEE?   HEAR?   TRY?

HOW?   WHEN?   WHERE?

PROJECTS

5.1 PROJECT PLANNING

Planning is something we all do almost instinctively in everyday life, as we prepare for a day trip, a night out, a dinner party or a wedding. Yet, work planning is notoriously poor in both the business and public sectors. The Channel Tunnel, for example, may have been a success from an engineering standpoint — the holes from England and France aligned within a half-meter's precision — but the cost of the project was nearly twice what was budgeted.

The 'Natural Planning' method is a brilliant approach advocated by productivity guru David Allen. The framework below is based on the same thinking and can be used to plan almost anything. The outcomes of the seven steps should be captured in a project plan, which then becomes a key reference for the team throughout the project.

PROJECT PLANNING

| 1. PURPOSE & VISION | 2. TASKS | 3. ACTION PLAN | 4. RESOURCES | 5. SCHEDULE | 6. MONITOR | 7. REVIEW |

PURPOSE AND VISION

A successful project starts with everyone being clear about its objectives and what must be delivered. Project managers should provide a vision of what the end result should look and feel like, and define the success criteria precisely.

TASKS

The next step is to brainstorm everything that might need to be done at any stage, in order to meet the project's objectives. At this early point in the process, don't drill down too specifically into what needs to be done, by whom and by when. What's important is to identify all the pieces of the jigsaw, even if it isn't obvious how they'll be put together. Once all the tasks are on the table, you can start sorting them into buckets that different people/teams can work on. You can then put the tasks into chronological order, providing a preliminary project timeline.

ACTION PLAN

The action plan captures who will do each task, and when. It should specify everyone who needs to be involved, and how. (Use the 'RACI' framework described in Section 5.2 if it's a complex undertaking.) It's crucial to identify what the very first actions need to be; deciding on further steps can often wait.

RESOURCES

The project leader needs to obtain estimates for the time and resources required and the associated costs. The plan should also highlight potential problems that might cause time or costs over-runs. The plan needs to say how each risk would be addressed and what will be done to make it less likely to happen in the first place. This is known as risk mitigation.

SCHEDULE

This specifies when each task will be started and finished, and when the start of a task depends on the completion of another. If complex, the schedule can be illustrated using a Gantt chart — a project management tool that graphically illustrates the schedule and how some activities depend on the completion of others — to make it easier to follow. Schedules often highlight key milestones along the way, such as when a whole phase of work is due to be completed or a prototype product will be ready for testing.

MONITOR

Project teams need to define how all parties will keep in touch, review progress, flag issues and resolve conflicts. Regular review meetings are often useful. The core team typically meets each week to determine whether everything is progressing as planned and on schedule, highlight any possible risks and decide what to do about them. Progress and actions can be recorded in a project status report — many templates are available online.

REVIEW

After the project has been completed, the team identifies what went well, what they'd do differently next time and how these lessons should be communicated to other parties that might benefit from them.

PROJECT RESPONSIBILITIES

With straightforward projects involving a small team, a basic action plan will capture who is responsible for completing each task and by when. With complicated projects involving multiple parties, the 'RACI' framework may be needed. It defines not only who is responsible for completing each element of a project, but also who's ultimately accountable for each task, and who needs to be consulted and informed as the work progresses.

CLARIFYING WHO DOES WHAT

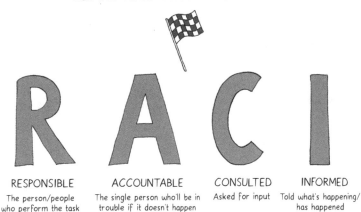

RESPONSIBLE	ACCOUNTABLE	CONSULTED	INFORMED
The person/people who perform the task	The single person who'll be in trouble if it doesn't happen	Asked for input	Told what's happening/ has happened

RESPONSIBLE

This means the person or people expected to perform all or part of the task.

ACCOUNTABLE

Being accountable for a task means that you take responsibility for the outcome, even if you have no hands-on involvement. Team leaders are accountable for the outcomes of all tasks performed by their team. US President Henry Truman had a sign on his desk saying, "The Buck Stops Here," to show that he, as chief executive, felt accountable for all policies put in place during his term in office.

CONSULTED

This includes people or teams that should be asked for advice and input on how a task should be completed. Consultation usually capitalizes on expertise from outside the team, but is also a good way of building awareness and acceptance of the project.

INFORMED

This specifies the people who need to be kept informed of decisions that might affect them, even if they aren't directly involved in decision-making.

RACIs are normally captured in a grid format. The example below highlights that the same people can perform multiple roles. It also shows that people informed about a task do not necessarily need to be consulted, and vice versa.

RACI GRID EXAMPLE

	TEAM/PERSON A	TEAM/PERSON B	TEAM/PERSON C	TEAM/PERSON D	TEAM/PERSON E	TEAM/PERSON F
TASK 1	R	R	A		C/I	C/I
TASK 2		R	A	C	I	I
TASK 3		A	R	C	I	I
TASK 4	C	R	R	R/A	I	
TASK 5				R	A	
TASK 6					R	A
ETC.						

5.3 PROJECT MEETINGS

At their best, project meetings are an opportunity to resolve difficulties and generate ideas far more effectively than would be possible from working in isolation. Unfortunately, they all too often absorb lots of time and yield little value. A meeting is most effective when everyone knows in advance what it's about, what they need to bring to the table and what must be achieved by the end of the session. When issuing an invitation, using the SPORT framework helps ensure that the meeting will be productive.

MEETING INVITATIONS

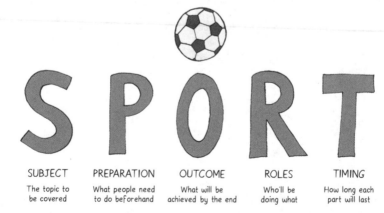

SUBJECT	PREPARATION	OUTCOME	ROLES	TIMING
The topic to be covered	What people need to do beforehand	What will be achieved by the end	Who'll be doing what	How long each part will last

A large part of working life is spent in meetings, so it's important that this time is used productively. A survey in 2018 for the *Independent* newspaper revealed that business meetings in the UK, France and Germany were far from optimal. Employees in these countries spent an average of 23 working days a year in meetings, and felt that nearly 60% of these were unproductive. Shockingly, nearly a quarter had witnessed someone falling asleep during a meeting. While business meetings are often scheduled for an hour or more, the consensus was that 40 minutes is the optimum length.

To ensure a productive project meeting, always have someone nominated as the chair, responsible for running it according to the tried and trusted process described below.

RUNNING AN EFFECTIVE MEETING

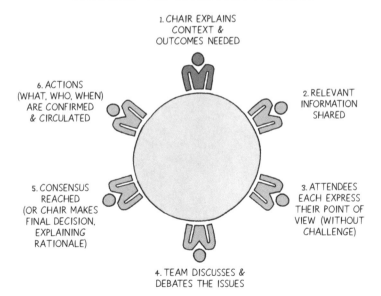

1. CHAIR EXPLAINS CONTEXT & OUTCOMES NEEDED

2. RELEVANT INFORMATION SHARED

3. ATTENDEES EACH EXPRESS THEIR POINT OF VIEW (WITHOUT CHALLENGE)

4. TEAM DISCUSSES & DEBATES THE ISSUES

5. CONSENSUS REACHED (OR CHAIR MAKES FINAL DECISION, EXPLAINING RATIONALE)

6. ACTIONS (WHAT, WHO, WHEN) ARE CONFIRMED & CIRCULATED

This process ensures that:

- The meeting remains focused on the desired outcomes
- Decisions are made after relevant information has been shared
- All attendees have the opportunity to put forward their point of view, without feeling intimidated
- There has been a thorough debate
- Decisions and actions are influenced by consensus

5.4 PROJECT COMMUNICATIONS

If you're leading a major project, you may need to consider how its progress and outcomes are communicated to key stakeholders and the wider community. If so, you will need to develop a communications strategy.

The framework below can be used to think through the communication needs for any project. The approach is based on the idea that for communication to be effective, the audience must want to do what you want them to do. It involves considering what people need to know, think and feel in order to be motivated to act in the desired way.

COMMUNICATION & INFLUENCE PLANNING

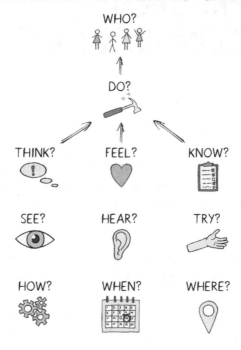

WHO?

DO?

THINK? FEEL? KNOW?

SEE? HEAR? TRY?

HOW? WHEN? WHERE?

WHO?

The start point is identifying the key stakeholders: those whose opinions are most important and whose actions will have the biggest impact on the success of the project.

DO?

The next step is to consider each stakeholder (or group of similar stakeholders) and decide what you want them to do as a result of the communication. Do you want them to make a certain decision? Advocate a course of action? Express a particular point of view in order to influence others?

THINK, FEEL AND KNOW?

This is the most important stage in the process. It requires putting yourself in the other person's shoes, and imagining what's actually important to them and what would make them want to act in the way you desire. Consider what they'd need to think and feel, and what new knowledge might help.

SEE, HEAR AND TRY?

The next step is to establish the experiences people need to have in order to think and feel in the desired way. What messages are relevant? Which media would work best? Do they need hands-on experience with something to shape their opinions?

HOW, WHEN AND WHERE?

The final step is to define the channels, develop the creative content and agree on the timeline that will deliver the communication plan most effectively.

COMMUNICATIONS PLAN TEMPLATE

Different Audiences	What do we want them to do?	What do we want them to think & feel to do this? What do we need them to know?	What's the best way to achieve this? (Approach? Message? Medium? Who best to deliver?)	When does this need to happen?	Who will prepare & who will deliver this?
etc.					

5.5 PROJECT REVIEWS

Project reviews are an excellent way for teams and organizations to learn from experience. Many of the world's most successful organizations subscribe to the concept of *Kaizen*, a Japanese business philosophy meaning 'change for good' or 'continual improvement.'

The author has a confession to make here. As a fan of the *Kaizen* principle, he hung a huge poster showing the text above from the ceiling of the office in order to inspire his teammates. Unfortunately — and quite embarrassingly — more than two years later he was told by a new team member from Japan that the poster had been hung upside down.

To improve over time, project leaders need to evaluate every piece of work and absorb learning that will help future projects run more smoothly and produce better end results.

Project reviews need not be complicated or overly time consuming. Team leaders should ensure that everyone feels comfortable offering frank feedback without fear of recrimination. People usually have a good idea of what did and didn't go well, so the review should focus on constructive suggestions and new ideas for what to do differently next time.

The review process requires team members to consider all aspects of the project — including outcomes, timing, costs and communications — and identify what they felt:

- Went particularly well
- Didn't go well
- Could be done differently in future

Ideally, the team should meet to share this feedback and then discuss and agree on changes to working practices for subsequent projects. Team members need to feel comfortable pointing out issues and be motivated to share their ideas on how things could be done better. Any team with this ethos is likely to succeed in the long run.

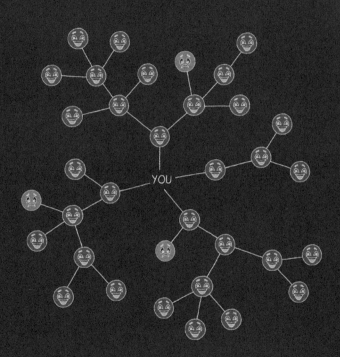

PART SIX

NETWORKS

6.1 NETWORK BUILDING

Many careers depend on having good business connections. This is particularly so as more and more people work as freelance contractors. Building a strong network is becoming increasingly important for professionals in every sector. Your network can help you to:

- Identify new business leads
- Publicize your products or services
- Build your professional knowledge
- Come up with and refine ideas
- Find new job opportunities

Here's how to gain a new contacts and build your network one person at a time:

GAINING A NEW CONTACT

REACH OUT TO AN
EXISTING CONTACT

ASK FOR AN
INTRODUCTION

BE FRIENDLY, CURIOUS AND
HELPFUL TO NEW CONTACT

REACH OUT TO AN EXISTING CONTACT

The best approach is to start with the people you know already. When you first enter the workforce, ask any family members or friends who work in a relevant field, or people you know from university, to help you start building your network. Or, contact professionals via social media, websites and email, explaining your passion for the area and offering your services for free in return for work experience. You just need to gain a few initial contacts, and then expand your network from there. If you obtain some paid work, ask your colleagues to suggest other people you could meet.

ASK FOR AN INTRODUCTION

Always ask for an introduction. If you approach someone you don't know without an introduction, you might get lucky, but 99 times out of 100, they'll ignore you. Just ask a contact to drop the person a line in advance, ask if it'd be OK for you to get in touch with them and explain why. Once you've got the green light, it's up to you to make a good impression.

BE FRIENDLY, CURIOUS AND HELPFUL

Section 6.3 describes in detail how to build rapport and trust, but applying a few basic principles will make a big difference. Business relationships work in the same way as any other relationship. If you're friendly, curious about the other person (see Section 2.3), honest and keep your promises, you're off to a great start. Ask how you might be able to help them, such as providing an introduction to others. Before the end of the meeting, invite them to get in touch with you at any time if they think you might be of service. It helps to be generous to the other person without expecting anything in return. In fact, they'll probably want to return the favour at some point due to 'the reciprocity principle' — the psychological norm of responding to a positive action with another positive action. After the meeting, find something to share with them that you think they'll find useful or might enjoy. It doesn't have to be business related; perhaps send a restaurant recommendation, a book or movie suggestion, or something associated with a personal interest they hinted at.

If you do these things as a matter of course, your network will expand rapidly, with each new contact potentially leading to several more contacts. Some recommendations will lead to a dead end, and don't expect to get on well with everyone you meet, but if you adopt this approach throughout your career, you'll create a large and valuable network.

BUILDING YOUR NETWORK

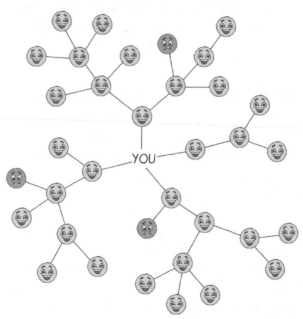

6.2 MEETING NEW CONTACTS

If meeting a new contact for the first time sounds like a daunting prospect, you can reduce the fear factor by following the guidelines below. The formula works well every time. It can also be easily adapted for an initial sales call or meeting.

MEETING A NEW CONTACT

Break the ice & thank

Say something about the (news) weather etc.

Ask where they're based etc.

(Thank) them for taking the time to meet you.

Context

XXXX suggested we meet to talk about (XX.)

They thought we should talk because...

What are your thoughts on XX?

Listen & find out about them

Why do you think that is?

Tell me about (your role)

How might I be able to (help you?)

Thank and clarify follow up

Thanks again for such a useful discussion.

I'll send through that article I mentioned.

To help ensure that the meeting goes well, do some homework on the other person. Take a look at their profile and recent posts on LinkedIn, Facebook, Instagram and YouTube, and search for them on Google to see what comes up. They'll appreciate it if you refer to something they've posted, published or said in a speaking engagement. And ask to connect with them on social media straight after the meeting.

The secret to success in any meeting like this is to get the person talking early on in the conversation. You need them to feel relaxed (see Section 6.3), and then use your listening skills (Section 2.3) to help them open up about themselves and their business priorities. Plan to talk for only a few minutes before asking them for their thoughts. When preparing for the meeting, find a way to explain the context succinctly and make it sound as relevant to them as possible.

You should aim to spend less than 30% of the time talking. Listen and probe for what the other person really needs and cares about. And then, if you think you might be able to help them, tell them how. Before ending the meeting, always try to agree on a follow-up of some sort (assuming you actually want to stay in touch). It doesn't matter how you reconnect; what's important is to secure a reason to continue the dialogue and provide another chance to strengthen your relationship.

6.3 BUILDING RAPPORT AND TRUST

When you meet someone, either virtually or in person, it's important to build rapport with them so they're more likely to want to work with you.

Here are three things you can do to establish rapport.

BUILDING RAPPORT

CATCH UP
FIRST

LISTEN
ACTIVELY

MIRROR
BEHAVIOURS

CATCH UP FIRST

Few people like to dive straight into business, although this varies a lot by individual (see Section 2.2). Most of us prefer to spend a few minutes getting to know each other or catching up about things that matter to us, such as family or mutual acquaintances. These kinds of exchanges are more natural when you're face to face, but are equally important at the start of virtual meetings. Spending a minute or so talking about topics other than work creates a relaxed, positive atmosphere. Start by asking the other person about how they are, and how work or life (depending on your relationship) is treating them. Talk about shared interests and experiences to create a connection. If you've met them before, show them that you remember, are interested in and can credibly discuss what matters to them.

LISTEN ACTIVELY

Share your thoughts on the topic that prompted the meeting, but don't talk much. Ask questions that prompt the person to tell you what's on their mind. Be genuinely interested in what they're saying and probe to understand their concerns. Almost everyone has hidden depths, and a story to tell, if you listen well (see Section 2.3). If meeting virtually, make sure their face is full-screen so you can see if they're interested in what you're saying and how they're reacting.

MIRROR BEHAVIOURS

When people get along, they mirror each other's behaviours. Mirroring happens naturally if you are in the moment and listening well. If you want someone to know that you like and respect them, however, you might make a conscious effort to mirror their actions. In virtual meetings, this means matching the volume, tone and language of their speech — don't use long words or technical jargon if they don't. Look at the camera because this gives the impression of eye contact. In face-to-face meetings, you might also consider copying their posture and mannerisms. People can't help but respond more positively to people who are more like themselves. Try to moderate your behaviour accordingly, while remaining true to your identity and avoiding coming across as insincere.

Building rapport helps you get a new relationship off on the right foot. Over time, you can earn the person's trust the same way you do among family and friends. The business world started talking about the 'Trust Equation' in 2000 after management expert David Maister featured it in his book, *The Trusted Advisor.*

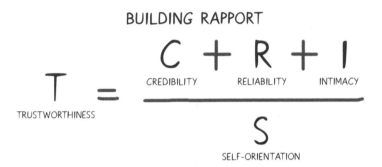

BUILDING RAPPORT

The equation represents some clever thinking, but most of us already understand the underlying concepts. The formula implies that you will earn someone's trust if you know what you're talking about (credibility), do what you say you'll do (reliability), act like a decent, honest human being (intimacy) and try to focus on their needs rather than your own (self-orientation). In other words, if you want to be trusted, be a trustworthy person. Here's a less mathematical way of thinking about how to earn trust:

HOW TO EARN TRUST

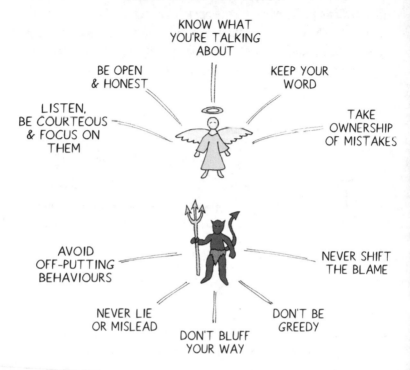

KNOW WHAT
YOU'RE TALKING
ABOUT

BE OPEN
& HONEST

KEEP YOUR
WORD

LISTEN,
BE COURTEOUS
& FOCUS ON
THEM

TAKE
OWNERSHIP
OF MISTAKES

AVOID
OFF-PUTTING
BEHAVIOURS

NEVER SHIFT
THE BLAME

NEVER LIE
OR MISLEAD

DON'T BE
GREEDY

DON'T BLUFF
YOUR WAY

6.4 HANDLING CULTURAL DIFFERENCES

If your work involves dealing with people from different countries, it helps to be aware of important differences between cultures. Making an effort to be knowledgeable about (and respect) differences will help you make a good impression and reduce your chances of committing a cultural faux pas. It's worth spending half an hour or so online to learn about a new culture before your first meeting. It needn't be all that in-depth, but it's worth understanding how business collaboration styles might differ from your own.

CULTURAL DIFFERENCES IN COLLABORATION STYLE

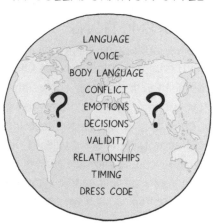

LANGUAGE
VOICE
BODY LANGUAGE
CONFLICT
EMOTIONS
DECISIONS
VALIDITY
RELATIONSHIPS
TIMING
DRESS CODE

LANGUAGE, VOICE AND BODY LANGUAGE

If English isn't the first language of the people you are meeting, be careful to:

- Use clear, straightforward English and accessible vocabulary
- Avoid idioms
- Be succinct
- Leave pauses to allow people to take in what you're saying
- Be patient and avoid interrupting when people are trying to find the right words

Even if everyone is speaking English, don't assume they're using words in the same way. 'Yes,' for example, might mean 'definitely' but could also mean 'I'll consider it.' The way people use their voice also varies by culture. A raised voice might signal aggression in the US, but in Latin America it might instead indicate passion for the topic. Body language, such as posture, facial expressions or hand waving, can be subtle or extremely obvious. Don't confuse a lack of expressiveness for a lack of enthusiasm, and be aware that your own body language may have a big influence on how others think and react. This is particularly true if you're meeting face to face.

CONFLICT AND EMOTIONS

When conflicts arise, addressing them openly may be entirely appropriate in the US or Europe. In Japan and China, though, arguments tend to be dealt with discreetly — possibly through written channels — to avoid confrontation and embarrassment. Similarly, asking about or expressing emotions, or discussing personal matters, is considered acceptable in some cultures but frowned upon in others. As such, take care to know the cultural norms and sense your audience before wearing your heart on your sleeve. Be careful if conversations turn to topics such as gender, sexuality, religion or politics. Attitudes may differ considerably from the people you normally talk to, so don't make any assumptions.

DECISIONS AND VALIDITY

Within the context of meetings, the way decisions are made may also be different from what you're used to. The boss's opinion might dominate the conversation until the required consensus is reached, or everyone might be asked their point of view and the decision made via a majority vote. The factors that are taken into consideration are another variable. Measurement and logical argument are considered paramount in some cultures; seniority, personal experience, intuition and historical perspectives hold more sway in others.

RELATIONSHIPS

If you're lucky enough to travel abroad for business, there are some additional considerations to be aware of. In some cultures, people prefer to establish relationships through social activity early in a collaboration, rather than letting them develop over time. This may mean, for example, that you're expected to have a relaxing meal — or multiple rounds of drinks — with business partners before getting down to business.

TIMING

Timekeeping for virtual meetings is more consistent across cultures, but it can vary much more when it comes to in-person meetings. If you're doing business in Ghana or Nigeria, for instance, you might hear locals use the phrase 'African time.' This refers to a generally looser adherence to schedules, versus the strict, clock-bound pace of things in Western countries. If you're used to meetings starting promptly and finishing on time, try to go with the flow if schedules end up being more fluid.

DRESS CODE

When visiting another country, it's important to consider how you dress. Be careful not to cause unintentional offense by your clothing or how you use your body to express yourself. In some parts of the world, it is illegal to wear revealing clothing or display affection in public, such as holding hands or kissing. Here are some of the many cultural differences related to the body that you should take into account:

CUTURAL DIFFERENCES RELATING TO THE BODY

In parts of Asia, the head is sacred and touching it, or passing something over it, is rude.

Avoid using hand signs (V-signs, thumbs up, OK sign, five fingers, making a fist, crossing fingers, pointing, etc.) because they may be highly offensive.

In many countries, people are expected to cover their arms & shoulders and most of their legs in churches and temples.

The left hand is seen as unclean in Islamic countries (& India), so shake hands and eat with your right hand.

People are expected to remove their shoes when entering homes or places of worship in many countries (and restaurants in Japan).

In much of Asia and North Africa, feet are seen as unclean, so avoid crossing your legs or pointing your feet towards someone.

The soles of the feet are seen as especially unclean, so keep them covered.

6.5 MAINTAINING RELATIONSHIPS

As your network grows, you'll need a system for remembering all your contacts and keeping track of what they're doing. A lot of people maintain a simple database to help them do this.

CONTACTS DATABASE

	CONTACT INFO	PREFERRED CHANNEL	HOW KNOW/MET	HOW WELL GET ON	INTERESTS/PASSIONS	KIDS?
JASMIN HAMILTON	XX@XX ETC.	LINKEDIN	UNI	9/10	TENNIS, BRIE, KOALAS	AMY (2015)
ADHIL FLETCHER	XX@XX ETC.	TEXT	MRS EVENT (2008)	7/10	SCI-FI, EXCEL	
ETC.						

If you are in your 20s or 30s, you may be thinking that there's no need to keep records of this nature. However, even the brightest minds can forget important details like these as they get older — or simply haven't had contact with someone for a number of years — so keeping notes at an early age is a good long-term investment.

Over the course of a career you're likely to work with ten to 20 people who end up knowing you quite well and are your most reliable advocates. There may be another few hundred allies who remember you quite well and know what a great job you do, and a further thousand or so distant associates who may remember your name but only have a vague impression, if any, of your abilities.

All three groups might be relevant to you at some point in your career. It pays to keep in regular touch with your inner circle of advocates and touch base with your allies every six months or so. You could put reminders in your calendar or set aside a couple of hours once a week to catch up with anyone you haven't been in touch with for a while. Try to think of something to tell them, or send to them, that's related to their job or one of their interests. This will remind them of your existence and how nice and helpful you are.

KEEPING IN TOUCH

KNOW WHAT INTERESTS THEM	SCHEDULE TIMES TO GET IN TOUCH	SHARE SOMETHING HELPFUL

It may be useful to maintain relationships with business associates in your outer circle as well. This can be done by following them on social media, 'liking' content of theirs that appeals to you, making occasional comments on their posts and re-sharing their content if you believe it might be relevant to your own connections. However, don't be tempted to endorse or share content indiscriminately, as this could damage your reputation and encourage your followers to ignore your posts or cut ties with you altogether.

PART SEVEN

90%

OF SEABIRDS
HAVE
PLASTIC
IN THEIR
STOMACHS

STORYTELLING

THE POWER OF STORIES

According to legend, the great writer Ernest Hemingway was lunching with a group of his literary friends in New York, and he agreed to a wager challenging him to write a story in just six words. Having secured bets of $10 each from his fellow diners, he finished his meal, took out a pen and jotted down a few words on a napkin. As the napkin was passed around the table, each of his guests gave a sigh of appreciation as they handed Hemingway his winnings.

For sale: baby shoes, never worn.

Ernest Hemingway

What is it about stories that make them so powerful? In *The Storytelling Animal*, the American literary scholar Jonathan Gottschall explains why stories are so important to the human species. He describes how early humans painted scenes onto cave walls showing how to hunt, and what appear to be warnings about potential conflict. Stories provide a safe environment to prepare for the world outside. They allow us to react to things and learn from them without actually experiencing them. Studies have shown that our brains respond in exactly the same way to stories as to the direct experience. Storytelling is at the heart of religion, education and even criminal investigation — detectives need to create plausible stories of what happened based on the available evidence. Stories are such an integral part of being human that we even weave them as we sleep.

Stories are even involved in how we process information. To take in what's going on around us, our brains have specialized centres to process different types of stimuli: one for visuals, one for sounds, one for movement, and so on. The brain then brings it all together and makes sense of it. In other words, we're wired to look out for and construct stories to enable comprehension. This is why storytelling is so valuable if we want people to take in what we're saying. It's particularly useful for turning complex information into something more digestible. A familiar story structure makes it easier for people to follow and understand the points being made, and string them together into something they can easily remember. Studies have even shown that information in the form of a story is scrutinized less and seen as more worthy of acting upon.

To succeed in business, you need to communicate your ideas in a clear and convincing way in meetings, presentations, customer calls, press interviews, investor briefings and on public stages. And so, storytelling is a skill every business professional should work on developing.

7.2 AUDIENCE AND MESSAGE

Before developing any story, you need to know your audience and the message you want to leave them with. As Ken Haemer, former Presentation Research Manager for AT&T Corp., put it, "Designing a presentation without an audience in mind is like writing a love letter and addressing it, 'To whom it may concern.'"

So, as with all communications plans (see Section 5.4), you should determine at the start:

- Who do I need to influence? What are their roles?
- Which decisions and actions do I need to affect?
- What single, overarching message do I need to deliver?
- Will the audience be receptive to the message or resistant to it?
- What do they already know about the topic? Do they know the back-story?
- Would they prefer to see the big picture and then debate the issues, or do they need to hear the full argument?

Putting yourself in your audience's shoes helps you choose the most suitable format for delivering the message, and the most effective way to tell the story. Presentations are particularly good for storytelling because they allow you to engage the audience directly, while other formats may be better for long, complicated stories or necessary for practical reasons. Whatever is needed, each format should be optimized based on how and when the audience will engage with it.

DELIVERY FORMATS

PRESENTATION

Optimize for attendees;
involve them in the performance.

REPORT

Optimize for reading;
make sure it stands alone.

INFOGRAPHIC

Optimize for a wider audience;
focus on visual impact & clarity.

DASHBOARD

Optimize for ease of use;
design around users and uses.

The next step is to take your overarching message and identify the three strongest supporting messages. Having four messages is acceptable, but 'threes' are lucky and magical, and good things come in them. This determines the content of the story you'll be developing later, so make sure you're happy with it before moving to the next stage.

MESSAGING FRAMEWORK

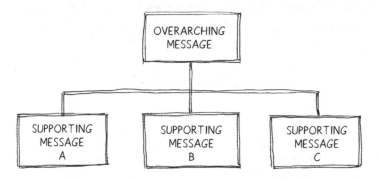

Being clear on these key messages means you have a ready-made 'elevator version' of your story — if you bump into the CEO in the lift and they ask you for your point of view, you'll be ready with a compelling 30-second overview. Here's an example of the how an elevator version neatly encapsulates a story's meaning.

THE STORY

Dear Kenji,

Remember a couple of weeks ago, when you came around to my house and my dad cooked for us? He told me later that when I went to the toilet, you swore at him and said he had a rubbish job. Also, when we went to the cinema on Friday, I felt really uncomfortable when you lied about finding a spider in your popcorn, so they'd give you another one for free. And yesterday, I was very upset when we argued, and you said I looked a like a rhinoceros and had the manners of a warthog. Well, for all these reasons, I've decided that you are a cruel, unpleasant person, and I don't want to spend another minute in your company.

Jodie

THE ELEVATOR VERSION

Kenji,

I'm leaving you because you:

1. *Were rude to my dad*
2. *Lied at the cinema*
3. *Insulted me*

Jodie

The next step is to flesh out your messaging framework by identifying all the points you need to make to create a convincing argument for each of your supporting messages.

MESSAGES & PERSUASIVE POINTS

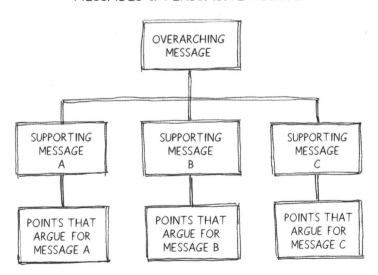

7.3 STORY STRUCTURE

Once you have established what you want to say, you need to find a compelling way to say it. We can turn to classic stories to understand how drama is created to keep audiences captivated. The 'Hero's Journey' is a structure seen in numerous legends, fairy tales and Hollywood movies, including *Star Wars*, *The Lion King* and *The Lord of the Rings*. Great business presentations, including TED Talks, are often inspired by this formula. It works the world over and provides an excellent template for injecting emotion into business communications.

THE HERO'S JOURNEY

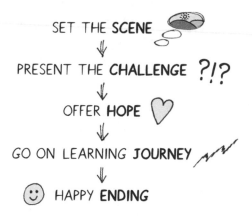

SET THE **SCENE**

↓

PRESENT THE **CHALLENGE** ?!?

↓

OFFER **HOPE** ♡

↓

GO ON LEARNING **JOURNEY** ⌇

↓

☺ HAPPY **ENDING**

SET THE SCENE

At the very start of these stories, everything is normal. There is a status quo that people are quite content with. Luke Skywalker is on the farm, the Hobbits are having a tea party, and your colleagues or clients are working in a business they're rightly proud of. Establishing what's good about *now* makes the audience care more about future threats.

PRESENT THE CHALLENGE

Nothing lasts forever. Whether you're in branding or in King's Landing, there's always a threat on the horizon or an opportunity you might seize too late. At this point in the story, it's important to highlight what's at stake. Our hero is not yet ready to be a hero. They are nervous and don't feel equipped to take on the challenge. This is where you come in.

OFFER HOPE

In a business context, your audience members are the nervous heroes, and you are Dumbledore, Gandalf and Obi wan Kenobi all rolled into one! It's your job to offer them hope and build their confidence. This means reassuring them that your proposals will help them succeed and reminding them how great success will feel when they achieve it.

GO ON LEARNING JOURNEY

In the next phase of the Hero's Journey, the protagonist goes through a series of trials, each of which builds their understanding, skills and belief. By the time they face the ultimate challenge, they're fully equipped and confident to overcome it (defeat Voldemort, destroy the Death Star or allow the Ring to fall into the fires of Mount Doom).

HAPPY ENDING

The battle's been won, the treasure's been found and the celebrations begin. While fireworks may breach health and safety regulations in a business environment, always end on a high note — in any experience, what people feel at the end is key to what they take away. When closing a presentation, for example, always provide a recap of the key learning and implications, make sure everyone knows what they need to do next, and leave them feeling confident that they're on the path to success.

By way of illustration, here's a summary of the benefits of storytelling in the form of the Hero's Journey, putting you in the role of the hero:

HERO'S JOURNEY ILLUSTRATION

You're great at your job. You've been doing it for a while and your ideas are well worth hearing.

But when you share your ideas, do people hang off your every word or do they switch off and go away unimpressed? It can be difficult to present your ideas compellingly, however good you are.

Thankfully, there is an approach you can use to ensure your presentations are amazing every time!

Follow the guidelines below and you'll soon learn everything you need to know.

In future, all your ideas will have the impact they deserve.

7.4 TELLING BUSINESS STORIES

Applying the 'Hero's Journey' structure to the messages you need to convey in a business presentation amplifies their impact and makes them more memorable. This takes time and space (and Post-It Notes). Keep trying different orders in which to present the points until you find a way that works best. Articulating the points out loud and taking another team member through the argument is a great way to identify the clearest flow and whether you need to add or subtract anything. Generally, if there are multiple ways to make the same point, pick the strongest and discard the others. Finally, add an introduction that outlines the context, the challenge and the key topics, and a close that helps the audience make the right decisions.

By the end of this process, you should have a storyline that includes all the points you want to make, from start to finish. The diagram below shows the flow of a storyline that's typical for a business presentation.

TYPICAL STORYLINE

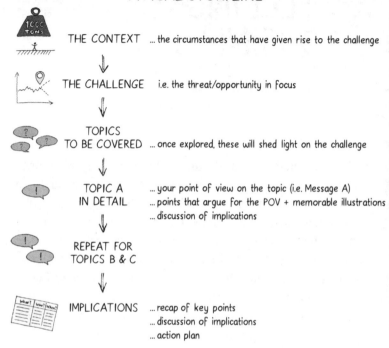

THE CONTEXT — ... the circumstances that have given rise to the challenge

THE CHALLENGE — i.e. the threat/opportunity in focus

TOPICS
TO BE COVERED — ... once explored, these will shed light on the challenge

TOPIC A
IN DETAIL — ... your point of view on the topic (i.e. Message A)
... points that argue for the POV + memorable illustrations
... discussion of implications

REPEAT FOR
TOPICS B & C

IMPLICATIONS — ... recap of key points
... discussion of implications
... action plan

The storyline should consist only of the basic points, described in words, without any details about how you are going to make them. Don't pile on facts, statistics, diagrams, etc., even if you already have some good ideas for them in mind. People often skip this step — laying out the basic storyline — and start creating a set of detailed slides, but if you can avoid the temptation to jump ahead, you'll save time later and produce a stronger final presentation.

When you're finally happy with your storyline, the next step is to decide how to bring each point alive in the clearest, most interesting and impactful way. Put a few heads together to help think things through if you can. Using a variety of approaches is a good idea because it will help you hold the audience's attention. Here are some ideas for how different points could be illustrated.

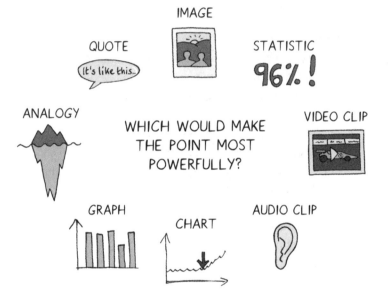

DECIDING HOW TO MAKE EACH POINT

IMAGE

QUOTE
It's like this..

STATISTIC
96%!

ANALOGY

WHICH WOULD MAKE
THE POINT MOST
POWERFULLY?

VIDEO CLIP

GRAPH

CHART

AUDIO CLIP

7.5 VISUAL DESIGN

Even if you've worked out a good way of making a point, how you decide to visualize it will dramatically affect its impact. The goal is to make it effortless for audience members to take in the idea. To do this, it helps to understand what happens in someone's brain during a presentation:

- If what's being shown and said aren't easily connected, the dissonance often results in neither being comprehended
- If it's hard to know where to look when shown something, attention will soon drift away
- If there's a lot of information to take in, the brain is likely to take in only some of it — not necessary the most important point

Visual design is crucial. Even the most cleverly constructed argument can fail to impress if the accompanying visuals fall flat or, worse still, actually detract from the message. If you're presenting a story, you don't necessarily need any visuals — a brilliant orator can command attention using their voice and personal presence alone (see Sections 8.4). Used well, however, visuals make the message easier to understand, remember and pass on.

PRINCIPLES OF GOOD VISUAL DESIGN

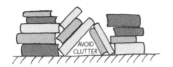

AVOID CLUTTER

~~DON'T BE VERBOSE;~~
~~TRY TO~~ USE AS FEW WORDS
~~AS YOU POSSIBLY CAN~~

KEEP PLENTY OF
BLANK SPACE

92%
PREFER
SIMPLE
DATA

USE SHADES OF ONE
COLOUR PLUS A
CONTRASTING COLOUR
TO DRAW THE EYE

CATCHY
VISUALS
MAINTAIN ATTENTION

MAKE SURE TEXT WILL BE READABLE

Key principles worth bearing in mind include:
- Focus on just one point at a time
- Keep the visuals as clear and uncluttered as possible
- Use as few words and numbers as you can
- Use colour and layout to draw attention to what's important
- Use eye-catching visuals at every opportunity
- Remove anything that doesn't contribute to the point or duplicates something else
- Make sure all text is readable

If you're not confident in this area, there is a fool-proof approach you could use. For each point you want to make, identify one simple supporting fact or figure and show it alongside a simple visual that dramatizes the point.

90%

OF SEABIRDS
HAVE
PLASTIC
IN THEIR
STOMACHS

Data is often important in business presentations, but nothing bores an audience more than being shown a page full of numbers. However, a well-chosen data chart can help highlight the underlying meaning. The graphic below shows some common chart types and how they should be used.

COMMON TYPES OF DATA CHART

For comparing figures
COLUMN

To show what's driving change
STACKED COLUMN

For ranking or long labels
BAR

Parts of a whole
DONUT

For comparing differences
FLAGPOLE

For comparing profiles
RADAR

For showing trends
LINE

For showing relationships
SCATTER

For plotting ups and downs
WATERFALL

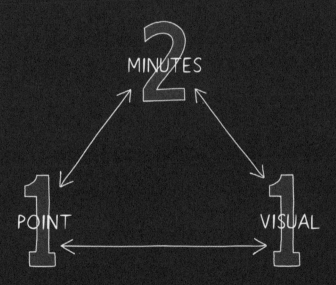

PART EIGHT

PRESENTATIONS

8.1 PRESENTATION SUCCESS FORMULA

At some point in your career, you'll probably be expected to make a presentation to your colleagues or clients. A well designed and delivered presentation is sure to impress, while a poor one may tarnish even the strongest reputation. It's not surprising that many people dread the prospect of taking centre stage to showcase their ideas.

Section 8.2 is designed to help you prepare for a presentation, and Sections 8.3–8.5 are about running it well. This section describes the general principles of effective presentations, starting with a formula for success.

GREAT PRESENTATIONS =

$$\frac{(YOU^2 + AUDIENCE) \times (STORY + ILLUSTRATION)}{(JARGON + WAFFLE)}$$

Great presentations depend the presenter. As Graham Staplehurst, Global Strategy Director at the consultancy Kantar, put it: "When you present, you need to be yourself, only more so." This is 'You' in the illustration above: it's you, but turbo-charged. In other words, presenters need to make a powerful connection with the audience, using the force of their personality. However, the impact of the message also depends on how relevant and compelling the story is, and how well it's brought to life through illustration (see Chapter 7). Even if the top half of the equation looks strong, a presentation's impact will be a fraction of what it could have been if the presenter loses the audience's attention by using jargon or starting to waffle.

The secret to a great presentation, therefore, is to:
- Find a way to establish trust and rapport with the audience, as early as possible
- Have a clear, well-structured story that includes convincing evidence and memorable illustrations
- Avoid using jargon and waffling at all costs

The look and feel of presentations varies depending on their objectives, the audience and the time available, but they typically follow the structure below.

TYPICAL PRESENTATION STRUCTURE

 WELCOME ATTENDEES
Greet everyone individually and create a connection with the group as a whole (e.g. via anecdote, humour).

 EXPLAIN RULES
Explain what's going to be covered, any house rules (e.g. phones/laptops off) and when questions are welcome.

 DELIVER PRESENTATION
Share point of view, backed up by evidence and brought to life with impactful illustration.

 STEER TOWARDS CONSENSUS
Recap key conclusions and discuss implications. Capture decisions and agreed actions.

 THANK & CLOSE
Thank everyone for attending and contributing to a successful outcome.

As the host of the meeting, it's your duty to ensure that all attendees have an opportunity to contribute to the discussion. The debate should not be dominated by a subset of individuals, however senior they are, so you may need to actively invite less-vocal participants to share their points of view before any conclusions are reached.

8.2 PREPARING FOR PRESENTATIONS

As with so many things in life, the secret to a successful business presentation lies in careful planning. A week or two before any presentation, make sure you've established the basics using the checklist below.

PRESENTATION PLANNING CHECKLIST

AUDIENCE?

Who is coming?
What will each person
need/expect?

TIME?

How long is the meeting?
Will there be 5+ mins
to set up at the start?

LOCATION?

Where is the
presentation
happening?

SPACE?

How large is the room?
Is there space to
move around?
Could we use the walls?

EQUIPMENT/TECH?

Screen for PC?
Video/tele-conferencing?
Wifi?
Flipcharts?

TAKE WITH US?

Infographics/posters?
Handouts?
Reports to take away?
Snacks?

Check these details with your colleagues and clients, and the venue if possible, so you can be thoroughly prepared. Of course, no plans are fool-proof, so you should also think through what you would do if something goes awry during your delivery.

When presenting virtually, anticipate how you'd pivot if you or attendees have technical difficulties. Could you switch to another communication channel? If it were audio only, how would you navigate this? At what point would you postpone the meeting? Do you know your material well enough to talk the audience through everything without any visual support?

PREPARING YOUR DELIVERY

As a rule of thumb, you should spend two to three times as long preparing your delivery as it will take to deliver it. It's quite helpful to rehearse what you are going to say out loud, either to yourself or, ideally, to someone else. This will help you identify any sections where your argument doesn't flow naturally, or that you need to refine and practise more, before you can deliver it with confidence. It's OK to write a script if this helps you clarify what you need to say, but never try to memorize it or read it word for word in front of your audience. If you do, the presentation will sound stilted and won't engage the listeners. When you're confident in your delivery, time how long it takes so that you can trim down the content if necessary. When deciding what to remove, a useful mantra is, 'If in doubt, leave it out!' Keep making changes until you are confident with everything you're going to say, or the audience will sense your lack of conviction and this will diminish your credibility.

TIMING

Most business presentations last for about an hour. You should plan to formally present for no more than 40 minutes and leave the remaining time for questions and discussion. Discussion can take place either at the end of the presentation or at various times within it. A helpful rule of thumb is that it takes about two minutes to communicate each point within your argument.

PRESENTATION TIMING

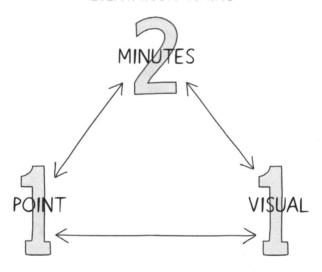

This means that an hour-long presentation should contain no more than about 20 points, and therefore no more than 20 visuals to support your points. When it comes to presenting, less is always more.

8.3 TAKING CHARGE

The most effective presenters strike a balance between making the audience feel included and relaxed, and radiating an air of quiet authority. Your presentations will be well received if you act as the host of the meeting, ensuring that everyone is well attended to and taking charge when necessary to keep everything on track.

HOSTING A PRESENTATION

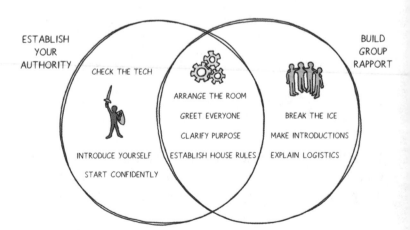

ESTABLISH YOUR AUTHORITY

CHECK THE TECH

INTRODUCE YOURSELF

START CONFIDENTLY

ARRANGE THE ROOM

GREET EVERYONE

CLARIFY PURPOSE

ESTABLISH HOUSE RULES

BUILD GROUP RAPPORT

BREAK THE ICE

MAKE INTRODUCTIONS

EXPLAIN LOGISTICS

CHECK THE TECH

For virtual presentations, or face-to-face sessions where you'll rely on electronic visual support, allow 15 minutes or so before the start to familiarize yourself with the equipment and make sure everything's working properly. If meeting in person, plan to arrive at least 30 minutes early, as there may be more to prepare before the first attendee arrives. Start by confirming that the technology works as expected because IT issues can take a while to resolve. Audiences will forgive minor hiccups, but significant problems will detract from your credibility and the presentation's impact. Make sure the room is neat and tidy, the lighting and air temperature are right, and the seating is well arranged. Everyone should have enough space to sit comfortably and see you, and any screens or flipcharts, without difficulty. You may need to move tables and chairs around until the space works.

WELCOME EVERYONE

As each attendee joins the meeting, say hello and exchange names if you haven't met before. Begin the presentation within a few minutes of the scheduled start time, but if someone joins late, take a second to welcome them too.

BREAK THE ICE

Start by thanking everyone for attending. The next few moments set the tone for the rest of the presentation, so it's worth thinking about and practising what you're going to say. A great presenter connects personally with everyone in the audience at the start. Telling a personal anecdote is one way of doing this. It doesn't need to be anything profound – it could just be some past connection you've had with the audience or the subject matter, or even something vaguely interesting that happened when preparing for the presentation or on the way to the venue. Think of something that should go down well with the audience and is very 'you.' Using humour can be particularly effective, but that can be difficult for some, and even the best-intentioned jokes may rub people the wrong way. The goal is to find an excuse to express your own personality; if you do, you'll find it easier to engage the audience for the rest of the presentation.

INTRODUCE YOURSELF

Start the formal part of the presentation by saying your name (even if you have already to individual participants), state what your role is and explain that you'll be leading the presentation.

CLARIFY PURPOSE

Briefly summarize the subject of the presentation and why it's important. Perhaps mention that with such an impressive combination of people, you're confident of a productive outcome. To manage expectations, you may also want to clarify topics that *won't* be covered, and how these areas can be discussed at a later date.

MAKE INTRODUCTIONS

People are more likely to make a positive contribution to a meeting if they introduce themselves and explain their role at the beginning. Surgical teams in hospitals, for example, are more likely to flag complications to the lead surgeon if they've declared their responsibilities before the start of the operation. Ask attendees to introduce themselves, unless everyone already knows each other well.

ESTABLISH HOUSE RULES

The rules you'd like the group to follow depend on your personal style and the nature of the gathering. It's usually appropriate to request that people avoid checking their phones during the meeting, and that they should let you know if they'll need to duck out for whatever reason. If there is a risk of time-consuming, off-topic digression, you might ask that questions be limited to points of clarification until the designated times for discussion (after each section, or at the end of the presentation).

EXPLAIN LOGICTICS

Explain how long the meeting will last and, if it's more than an hour, when there will be breaks. Check if anyone will need to leave before the end of the presentation. By doing this, anyone who must leave early will feel at ease and the remaining attendees will have implicitly agreed to stay for the duration. It also gives you the chance to make adjustments to your presentation if necessary – to cover a topic or summarize the conclusions, for example, before a key audience member has to leave.

PROJECT CONFIDENCE

Section 8.5 provides guidance on how to deliver presentations that engage the audience, but nothing is more important than your first few sentences. Keep working on what you're going to say at the very start, until you're sure it will come across well. The confidence this gives you will last until the end of the presentation. You'll also ooze confidence if you use your voice to engage your audience and convey your message powerfully. Speech variation is key. Skilled presenters can gain, hold and regain attention by changing their volume, pace and pitch and using pauses deliberately.

USING YOUR VOICE

VOLUME	PACE & PITCH	PAUSES

VOLUME	PACE & PITCH	PAUSES
Loud enough to hear easily	Avoid tendancy to talk quickly	Use deliberate, frequent pauses
Louder for emphasis	Vary pace & pitch to engage	... easier to take in
Quieter for suspense	Slower & lower for emphasis	... creates emphasis
	Faster & higher for excitement	... shows confidence

Be aware of the speed at which you speak. In a stressful situation you will naturally speak faster, so make sure you take a breath, pause and speak more slowly. This is especially important if any audience members have a different first language.

Here are some other useful techniques to use during your delivery, some of which you may need to practise in advance:

- For each point, identify the key words or phrases that will help the audience understand and remember it
- To make your delivery sound natural, imagine you're addressing each point to an individual audience member
- Explain essential technical terms and avoid unnecessary jargon and acronyms
- Speak more slowly and in a lower voice to emphasize a point; talk faster and at a higher pitch to create excitement
- When you're making an important point, raise your volume a little, then pause for a few moments to allow the significance of what you've said to sink in

- Pauses also give you time to think and help you control your rate of speech
- In face-to-face meetings, if people are talking among themselves, simply pause, look at them with a neutral face and wait for them to stop. If they don't take the hint, say something like, 'Is there an issue you'd like to discuss?'

8.4 PRESENTING FACE TO FACE

If you have the opportunity to deliver a presentation face to face, you can make your presence felt and command your audience's attention not only by what you say and show, but how you use your body.

USING YOUR BODY

 SMILE A LOT

 MAKE EYE-CONTACT WITH EVERYONE, EVERY SO OFTEN

 STAND TO COMMAND AUTHORITY

 SIT TO BE PART OF THE TEAM (E.G. DURING DISCUSSION)

 WAVE YOUR ARMS IF IT'S NATURAL; DON'T CROSS LIMBS

 IF STRESSED, PAUSE, TAKE A BREATH & SLOW DOWN

 IF YOUR MOUTH'S DRY, BITE YOUR TONGUE AT THE BACK

SMILING

As a first step, just be yourself and focus on smiling. Smiling makes people warm up to you, want to listen to what you're saying and be supportive. Your voice really does sound more inviting and engaging when you have a smile on your face. This is relevant in virtual presentations but is even more powerful face to face.

MAKING EYE CONTACT

It's also important to make eye contact with your audience. From time to time, spend a moment or two looking at each person's face, turning towards the person most relevant to what you are saying if you can. Avoid looking only at one member of the audience, although it may be worth having slightly more eye contact with the most influential people.

STANDING OR SITTING

You can either stand or sit, depending on what's appropriate for the occasion and what feels right. Standing boosts your sense of authority, whereas sitting is better if you want to foster a sense of collaboration. Some presenters prefer to stand at the start of a presentation but sit down later on when everyone is sharing their perspectives or discussing the implications. When standing, avoid shuffling around because this can look awkward and be distracting. It's fine to walk around a bit as you present, and it can heighten attention, but make sure your movements look purposeful. When sitting, try not to fidget. If it's obvious that you can't help making certain movements, audiences will quickly ignore them. If not, they may be off-putting.

WAVING YOUR ARMS

Presenters are sometimes told to not wave their arms, but this is not necessarily good advice. In general, do what feels natural because it will make you feel confident and help you express enthusiasm for what you're saying. Wave your hands and arms around if it that's what you naturally do, but reel them in if there's a risk of coming across as manic. If you feel there's an issue with overly dramatic gestures, aim to make small adjustments over time to improve how you come across.

COPING WITH STRESS

Even experienced presenters can feel stressed from time to time. If you start feeling uptight, take one or two deep breaths and a drink of water before continuing. Remind yourself that everyone in the room whose opinion counts knows that presenting is difficult and wants you to succeed. If your mouth gets dry and you don't have any water, gently bite the back of your tongue — this will generate saliva and provide quick relief.

8.5 INVOLVING THE AUDIENCE

There are few bigger wastes of time in business than a dull presentation. The audience struggles to pay attention and takes in little of the content. One of the most effective ways to ensure that people stay alert is to actively involve them in the proceedings. Here are a few ideas for getting attendees to participate.

PARTICIPATION TECHNIQUES

ASK NEEDS
UPFONT

INVITE
QUESTIONS

ASK
QUESTIONS

ASK TO PREDICT IN HEAD
BEFORE YOU EXPLAIN

ASK FOR A
VOLUNTEER

DEVISE A
MINI QUIZ

Asking each audience member in turn to say what they hope to gain from the meeting has several benefits:

- It gets everyone talking early on, which sets the tone for an open, discursive meeting
- It helps people feel more invested in the meeting
- It allows you to tailor what you say to what attendees care most about
- It can be used as a checklist at the end to make sure the content and discussion have addressed everyone's needs

This technique is particularly valuable if you ever find yourself expected to deliver a presentation without having been given a proper brief. You'll still have to think on your feet, but it's better to know at the start what people are hoping to learn — and re-set expectations early on — than deliver stiff, cut and dried content to an increasingly frustrated audience.

Inviting questions and posing them to the audience are good ways to add variety to your delivery. When faced with a question, our brains instinctively try to answer it. That's why asking questions is such an effective way to engage an audience.

A common fear of presenters is that they'll be asked a question they can't answer. How you handle questions will obviously affect your credibility, so before a presentation, try to think of all the questions that could come up and figure out how you'll handle them. If you're asked something you hadn't anticipated, do your best to answer it, but be honest if you can't. Do not attempt to bluff your way out of it. Here are some tips for handling tricky questions.

HANDLING QUESTIONS

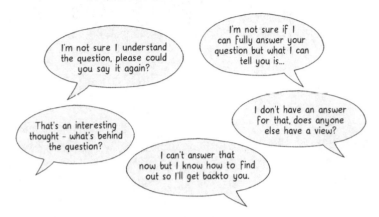

Sometimes, the discussion around a question can go on too long or become irrelevant. Use your judgment on whether to let the debate run its course or call a halt to the discussion so more important topics can be covered. A good way of doing this politely is to say something like, 'This is clearly an important discussion to be had at some point, but in the interests of time, I'd like to suggest that we focus back on X.'

If you want to take audience engagement to the next level, you can ask someone to be actively involved in demonstrating a point. In a virtual presentation, this might involve trying out a demo of a new product or technology as the audience watches. In a face-to-face presentation, it could mean asking someone to play the role of the glamorous assistant. For example, to make the point that bombarding people with messages results in a lack of focus, ask a volunteer to try to catch as many ping-pong balls as they can, and then throw 20 at them simultaneously from a bucket. They probably won't catch any. Simple moments of theatre like this energize the audience and make the presentation more impactful and memorable.

PART NINE

FIND YOUR 'HERD'  PAPER GIRAFFE

CLAPPING GAME  ROCK, PAPER, SCISSORS

WORKSHOPS

WORKSHOPPING PRINCIPLES

Workshops are typically longer than other meetings and serve a different purpose. They're ideal for solving specific problems or developing strategies that require input from a specific combination of people. Workshops often involve 4–14 people, are frequently held at an offsite location and can last anywhere from a few hours to several days. These deep-dive sessions work well for addressing the types of challenges the business has faced before.

Before starting any detailed planning, however, you should ask yourself whether a workshop is the right thing to do. Bringing together a group of experts for hours, or even days, is a major time and cost commitment. So, only decide to run a workshop if you're convinced the topic is important enough to warrant it, and that the group input and interaction is necessary. If the problem to be solved is complex and hard to define, you may need to adopt a more agile approach.

With a skilled facilitator, workshops can be adapted on the fly to explore unexpected themes should they emerge, but as a starting point, they generally follow the outline shown below.

TYPICAL WORKSHOP COMPONENTS

EQUIP	INSPIRE	GENERATE	PRIORITIZE	PLAN
Provide essential knowledge	Showcase brilliant examples	Come up with and refine ideas	Identify ideas worth pursuing	Agree who will do what, by when

EQUIP

At the start of the workshop (or beforehand) it's important to bring all attendees up to a minimum level of knowledge about the topic. This should include an explanation of the business issue, the context, why the challenge must be met and what success would look like. This ensures that everyone understands why the workshop is being conducted and what needs to be achieved by the end of it.

INSPIRE

Workshops typically involve at least one session designed to provide inspiration, to help participants get into the right mindset and to get their creative juices flowing. This might include examples of how other businesses have addressed a similar challenge. Bringing in guest speakers with relevant stories to tell can be particularly effective.

GENERATE

Workshops allow the right combination of people to collaborate and generate new ideas. Giving participants time and space to interact leads to imaginative solutions. Workshops should therefore involve activities that inspire creativity and encourage collaboration. The ideas can then be built on and refined collectively.

PRIORITIZE

In a workshop setting, every participant's opinion is important. When it comes to identifying priorities, a democratic vote is the norm. Once the most promising ideas have been agreed upon, the team can decide which should be leveraged immediately and which can be developed later on.

PLAN

As with any business meeting, workshops should finish with agreement on an action plan. A key output from a workshop is a record of who is going to do what, and by when, to move the ideas forward.

9.2 VIRTUAL WORKSHOPS

Virtual workshops allow people from different locations to collaborate in a safe, cost-effective way. The same core principles apply regardless of whether a workshop is virtual or in person, but if you're used to the face-to-face version, running an effective session online requires a few important adjustments.

EFFECTIVE VIRTUAL WORKSHOPS

SHORT
DURATION

PRECISE
AGENDA

CLEAR HOUSE
RULES

VERBAL
ICEBREAKER

REGULAR
BREAKS

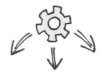

BREAKOUT
SESSIONS

SHORT DURATION

In-person workshops can run all day, but people find it harder to maintain focus for that long when staring at a computer screen for a virtual meeting. Online workshops should last no longer than about four hours. If more time is needed, the sessions should be spread across multiple days.

PRECISE AGENDA

In virtual workshops, facilitators are not in control of the physical environment and cannot engage, encourage and control people using eye contact and body language. What the facilitator says, and their tone of voice, are paramount (see Section 8.3). Working remotely also makes it harder for participants to concentrate. There are likely to be more distractions — from children, pets, washing machines, delivery drivers, etc. — and participants may be tempted to multi-task. Facilitators therefore need to direct proceedings with greater precision and authority.

CLEAR HOUSE RULES

At the start of a virtual workshop, facilitators need to ensure that all participants are familiar with the functionality of the platform and aware of the house rules everyone's expected to follow. Facilitators should:

- Ask everyone to keep their cameras on, explaining that this helps foster a collaborative spirit that's key to the workshop's success
- Request that people keep their microphones muted, apart from when they're talking, to minimize background noise
- Encourage participants to be in 'do not disturb' mode (avoiding calls and messages, and switching off notifications) and explain that there will be regular breaks for people to respond to anything urgent

- Demonstrate how to use specific features of the virtual meeting platform that are integral to the workshop

VERBAL ICEBREAKER

An icebreaker is arguably even more important for an online workshop than an in-person session. The question-and-answer icebreaker described in Section 9.4 works particularly well in on online environment.

REGULAR BREAKS

Since energizers are difficult to orchestrate virtually, participants should be encouraged to stretch their legs and grab some fresh air during the scheduled breaks. Given that people find it hard to concentrate for long periods when they're engaged remotely, breaks should be fairly frequent; ten minutes every hour should be sufficient.

BREAKOUT SESSIONS

If the workshop has more than about eight participants, you might want to use breakouts involving two to five people at certain points. Breakouts are ideal for:
- Getting to know one another other better
- Discussing a specific topic in depth
- Developing a prototype to share with the wider group
- Brainstorming how to make an existing idea better

9.3 WORKSHOP PLANNING

If you have never planned a workshop before, it can be an intimidating prospect, but this step-by-step process will set you off in the right direction.

DEFINE OBJECTIVES

Write down why you need a workshop, what you aim to achieve by the end if it and the tangible outputs that will be produced.

IDENTIFY ATTENDEES

Who has to be there to achieve these objectives? What is the smallest possible group? Who else would contribute relevant knowledge or creativity? For larger groups, retreat-like events can be organized that utilize many of the same principles and techniques as workshops, but these require advanced logistical skills and bigger budgets.

CHOOSE DATE(S), DURATION AND LOCATION

You'll almost certainly need to revise these later as you plan in more detail, but it's helpful to have ideas in mind at the start. The best locations have plenty of space, natural light and an uplifting, creative atmosphere.

OUTLINE OF SESSIONS

Working back from the desired outcomes, think of the main 'chunks' that will need to be included in the workshop. Then, for each of those segments, figure out what the session with involve, including the co-creation activities it should include (see Section 8.5).

ICEBREAKERS, ENERGIZERS AND BREAKS

To help attendees stay alert, creative and motivated throughout the workshop, you'll need to include an icebreaker at the start and energizers every few hours (see Section 8.3). Allow time for 15-minute breaks about every hour and a half.

DETAILED AGENDA

A detailed agenda helps orientate participants and makes it easier to stick to the schedule. Below is an example of an agenda for a one-day workshop. This template is for a workshop in which participants need to be equipped with a lot of information before they can begin brainstorming, which won't always be necessary.

EXAMPLE WORKSHOP AGENDA

		LED BY	MATERIALS NEEDED
8.45	Coffee		Coffee & breakfast foods
9.00	Welcome	Host	
9.15	Icebreaker	Facilitator	Icebreaker materials
9.30	Objectives for day & house rules	Facilitator	Laptop/screen + flip chart
9.45	Equip/inspire Session 1	Speaker 1	Laptop/screen
10.15	Break		Coffee, etc.
10.30	Equip/inspire Session 2	Speaker 2	Laptop/screen
11.00	Equip/inspire Session 3	Speaker 3	Laptop/screen
11.30	Energizer + break	Facilitator	Energizer materials; coffee etc.
11.45	Generate Session	Facilitator	Post-Its + pens
1.00	Lunch		Lunch foods
1.30	Prioritize Session	Facilitator	Flip chart + Post-Its
2.00	Sub-group planning sessions	Sub-groups	Flip charts (one per group) + pens
3.00	Energizer + break	Facilitator	Energizer materials; coffee, etc.
3.15	Plan sharing	Sub-groups	Flip chart
3.45	Likes & builds	Other sub-groups	Flip charts + pens
4.15	Final action planning	Facilitator	Flip chart + pen
4.30	Close	Host	

A useful rule of thumb is that at least 20% of the time should be spent doing something easy or fun, leaving the remaining time for serious matters.

IDEAL WORKSHOP RATIO

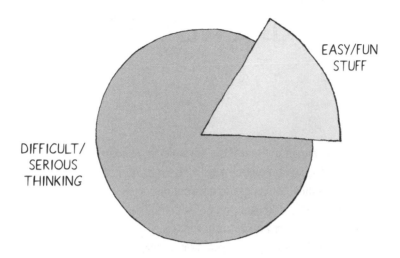

EASY/FUN
STUFF

DIFFICULT/
SERIOUS
THINKING

This means either having plenty of breaks and energizers or, better still, creating an agenda that includes regular interactive sessions, discussions, Q&As, quizzes or other diversions.

9.4 ICEBREAKERS AND ENERGIZERS

Icebreakers are short, interactive sessions at the start of a workshop, offsite meeting or conference, designed to get attendees into the right mood for creative thinking and collaborative work. A good icebreaker helps people get to know each other, communicate more freely and foster a spirit of shared purpose. There are hundreds of great ideas online for both small groups who already know each other quite well and larger groups of colleagues and strangers. Choose whichever icebreaker feels right, given the numbers of attendees and what you know of their personalities. Participants should all feel comfortable with whatever the icebreaker requires them to do, but ideally, they should also feel slightly nervous or excited.

The simplest icebreakers require each participant to share something about themselves with the group. These work well in both virtual and face-to-face workshops. For example, the facilitator could ask each attendee one of the following questions, picked at random:

- As a child, what did you want to be when you grew up?
- What was the naughtiest thing you did as a child?
- Where is the furthest from home you've been?
- Are you better at drawing, running or cooking?

- Which is bigger, your shoe size or the age you first moved house?
- What are you most scared of?
- Where in the world do you most want to visit?
- When was the last time you laughed really hard?

These questions work well because people have to give some thought to their answer but can usually respond without too much difficulty. They can either decide to go for a safe response or to say something more surprising. The questions themselves are only the starting point. Like a game show host, it's up to the facilitator to ask questions that encourage participants to get into the swing of things and reveal more about themselves.

Here are four reliable icebreakers that work well for face-to-face workshops:

ICEBREAKERS

3 THINGS IN COMMON

Split into groups of 3-6 people you don't know well. Find 3 things you all have in common.

WINNER GOES BACKWARDS?

Split into groups of 3-6 people you don't know well. Find 3 sports in which the winner goes backwards

WHICH ARE YOU?

Move to opposite sides of the room depending on whether you are/prefer...

City or country? Beach or mountain? Morning or evening? Elvis or the Beatles? Sibling(s) or only child? Left or right handed? Etc.

SPEED DATING

Set up pairs of chairs opposite each other in a large circle and ask everyone to sit and talk with the person opposite for 3 mins. Then rotate the outer ring by one and repeat until they've gone full circle.

Energizers are short activities designed to refresh workshop participants mentally and physically. They're worth including in both virtual and face-to-face workshops. Plan on running an energizer every three to four hours, or more often if the session is virtual or confined to a single room. Energizers that involve moving around are ideal because people can become stiff and uncomfortable if seated for too long, and even the mildest exercise can help restore mental agility.

VIRTUAL ENERGIZERS

There are hundreds of great energizers described online. Thiagi. com and Hyperisland.com are excellent resources for these. Some involve physical interaction, and are therefore only suited to face-to-face workshops, but the majority work equally well virtually. If you visit these sites, recommended energizers for virtual workshops include: 'Looking Around,' 'Story Around a Circle,' 'Shake Down' and 'Touch Blue.'

FACE-TO-FACE ENERGIZERS

In face-to-face workshops, energizers can exploit the physical proximity of attendees to amplify energy levels. Obviously, you need to be mindful of the physical abilities of those attending, and it's best to avoid activities that require significant physical contact. Here are four examples:

ICEBREAKERS

FIND YOUR 'HERD'

PAPER GIRAFFE

CLAPPING GAME

 ROCK, PAPER, SCISSORS

FIND YOUR HERD

Ask everyone to think of a farm animal and start making its noise. Their task is to find the rest of their 'herd' by moving around the room and listening. This energizer may not be suitable for all audiences, but it tends to create lots of laughter and energy.

PAPER GIRAFFE

Ask participants to hold a piece of A4 paper behind their back and, without looking, tear it into the shape of a giraffe. Then, ask everyone to show what they produced, celebrating the unique charm of each brave attempt.

CLAPPING GAME

Most people remember how to play this from childhood. You clap your own hands together, clap with your partner using right hands, go back to your own two-hand clap, and then clap with your partner using left hands. The pattern is repeated, faster and faster.

ROCK, PAPER, SCISSORS

This old childhood game works well as a tournament, especially with large groups. Each round is 'best of five', with the winner moving on to compete with another winner and the loser following them and cheering them on in subsequent rounds.

CO-CREATION ACTIVITIES

One of the main advantages of bringing people together in a workshop is that you can use their collaborative creativity to generate lots of ideas quickly and their collective intelligence to identify the right ones to take forward. However, it's important that people initially generate ideas on their own before these are shared with the group because this results in greater diversity of thought. It also ensures that the forceful individuals do not inhibit contributions from everyone else. After everyone's thoughts have been aired — without interruption or judgment — the team can then work collaboratively to build on each other's ideas and identify the gems.

There are many techniques you could use to help people come up with good ideas. *The Ideas Book*, by marketing consultant Kevin Duncan (from the same series as this book), is an excellent source of inspiration. If you're new to facilitating workshops, you could try the technique described below. It's easy to manage and works reliably.

FOOLPROOF CO-CREATION EXERCISE

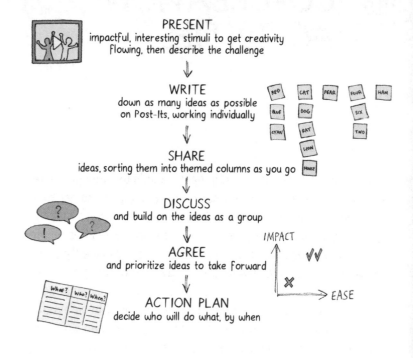

PRESENT
impactful, interesting stimuli to get creativity
flowing, then describe the challenge

WRITE
down as many ideas as possible
on Post-Its, working individually

SHARE
ideas, sorting them into themed columns as you go

DISCUSS
and build on the ideas as a group

AGREE
and prioritize ideas to take forward

ACTION PLAN
decide who will do what, by when

This approach isn't too time consuming because the ideas are shared with the group and sorted into themes at the same time. As facilitator, ask a participant to read out one of their ideas, and then decide whether it represents a new thought or is just another way of expressing something that's already been mentioned. If in doubt, ask the whole group whether they think it is an original idea; the debate at this point can be valuable.

The next stage is an open discussion about the themes that have been identified, exploring which ideas have most potential and why. Try to ensure that all attendees have the chance to share their thoughts. Sometimes a clear winner will emerge quickly, but if there are several promising ideas, you can use the matrix below to help with prioritization. Take each theme in turn, asking the group to assess its likely business impact and how easy it would be to implement. The goal is to identify themes that score well on both dimensions, and the discussion around this will bring to light some of the implementational consequences of the different options.

OPTION PRIORITIZATION MATRIX

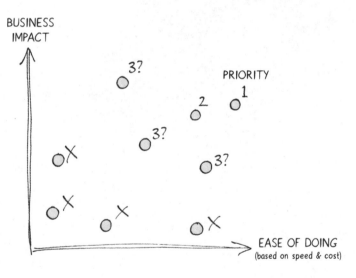

Once the whole group has identified the priorities, action plans for each priority can be developed collectively or in relevant sub-teams. These plans can then be shared, discussed and improved by the whole group, and next steps documented.

PART TEN

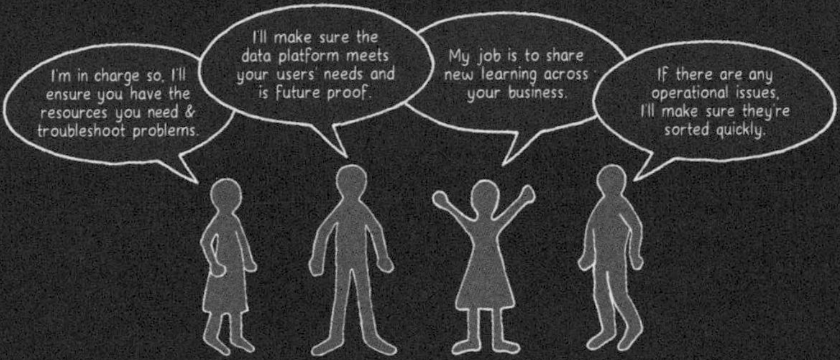

PITCHES

10.1 PITCH DEVELOPMENT PROCESS

For many companies, winning new business on a regular basis is essential. For continued success, it's important to convert a good percentage of opportunities into revenue-generating business. However, pitch development can be time consuming and expensive, so not every opportunity is worth the investment. To determine how much time and money to spend on a pitch, estimate the size of the prize and your likelihood of success.

OPTION PRIORITIZATION MATRIX

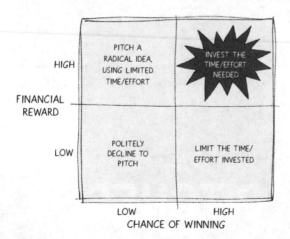

New business pitches typically involve at least two phases. In the first phase, the client issues a brief to several potential suppliers, requesting a written proposal from each of them. Companies submitting the most promising proposals are then invited to present their ideas in the second phase. The flow chart below outlines what pitching usually involves.

PITCH DEVELOPMENT PROCESS

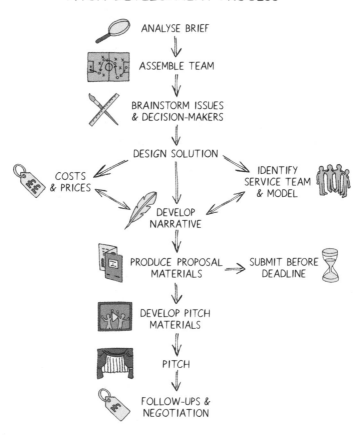

ANALYSE BRIEF

ASSEMBLE TEAM

BRAINSTORM ISSUES & DECISION-MAKERS

DESIGN SOLUTION

COSTS & PRICES

IDENTIFY SERVICE TEAM & MODEL

DEVELOP NARRATIVE

PRODUCE PROPOSAL MATERIALS → SUBMIT BEFORE DEADLINE

DEVELOP PITCH MATERIALS

PITCH

FOLLOW-UPS & NEGOTIATION

The first step is to review the brief and decide whether or not to submit a bid. Consider what would be required to develop a strong pitch and deliver a successful project. If you believe you could do both, the next step is to bring together the pitch team. This could be any number of people, depending on the size and complexity of the project, and may require the help of external partners. Once assembled, the team needs to identify who within the client's organization will ultimately decide whether to hire you or a competitor. The team must then establish the key needs relating to the brief of each decision-maker (see Section 10.2).

The next stage is designing the solution. Complex projects may require you to estimate and re-estimate the cost of different product or servicing scenarios that would appeal to the client. Once the team has agreed on what to propose, the next step is to develop a narrative that communicates the proposal in a powerful way (see Sections 10.3 and 10.4) before the proposal document is produced and sent to the client.

If invited to take part in the second round, involving an in-person or virtual pitch presentation, another phase of work begins. Presenting content taken directly from the proposal document will rarely be effective, so the team needs to devise a presentation that brings the ideas to life (see Chapters 7 and 8).

If the client is interested in working with you, you'll usually need to negotiate more detailed expectations, terms and conditions before finalizing the deal. Whenever you quote a price, be sure to spell out exactly what the client will receive, including any assumptions you've made. Avoid simply reducing the price to close the sale, unless this amounts to just 2–3% as a 'goodwill' gesture. Instead, explore scenarios involving cost-saving changes to what the client would receive, or the speed of delivery, in order to offer a lower price.

10.2 UNDERSTANDING DECISION-MAKING

When you're pitching for new business, it is essential to identify who will make the ultimate buy decision, and who else will have a major influence on that call. There are usually only two or three individuals with genuine clout, and establishing who they are is key to a successful close. The person responsible for arranging the pitch may not be a key decision-maker, but if you've built a good rapport with them (see Section 8.4), they should be able to tell you who's in charge.

> Individuals make decisions, not businesses.

Once you know who the decision-makers are, you need to find out as much about them as possible. Search for them on Google, LinkedIn and other social media platforms, and read their recent posts, articles and endorsements. Try to find out what they're interested in, their views on relevant topics and what they are like as a person (see Section 2.1).

How decision-makers actually make decisions is complicated, and varies from one person to the next, but here are some of the factors that are often part of the mix:

FACTORS AFFECTING SUPPLIER DECISIONS

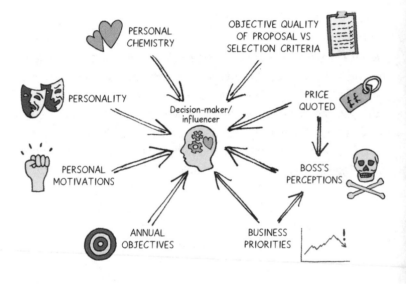

The more you understand about the decision-makers, the better positioned you'll be to develop a proposal that will appeal to them. If possible, arrange to meet them in person so you can get to know them, and use your listening skills (see Section 2.3) to find out as much as you can about the areas illustrated above. If you don't have a chance to actually meet them, talk to anyone who knows them and try to glean as much insight as possible.

The next stage of the process is to figure out the three or so client needs that the successful pitch must address more effectively than competitors' pitches. It can be helpful to run a brainstorm session, using the process below, to identify these key needs. This should involve everyone who knows the client.

PITCH BRAINSTORM

FIRST THIRD OF MEETING...

WHAT ARE THE REAL ISSUES BEHIND THE BRIEF?
HOW DOES IT RELATE TO WIDER COMPANY ISSUES?
WHAT MATTERS MOST TO THE BUSINESS?

SECOND THIRD OF MEETING...

WHO ARE THE REAL DECISION-MAKER(S)?
WHAT DO THEY THINK, FEEL, WANT?
WHAT MATTERS MOST TO THE DECISION-MAKER(S)?

FINAL THIRD OF MEETING

WHAT 3 NEEDS SHOULD WE BASE OUR PROPOSAL ON?
HOW ARE WE UNIQUELY WELL PLACED TO MEET THESE NEEDS?

10.3 PROPOSAL CONTENT

Proposal documents need to be easy to follow and communicate clearly how the solution answers the brief. The structure below is a useful starting point for business-to-business proposals.

PROPOSAL STRUCTURE

SUMMARY

BUSINESS CONTEXT &
CHALLENGES A, B & C

HOW WE'D HELP YOU ADDRESS A...
& WHY WE ARE UNIQUELY WELL
PLACED TO DO SO

REPEAT FOR B & C

OVERVIEW OF
PROPOSED SOLUTION

TEAM & SERVICING

FUTURE PROOFING

INVESTMENT OPTIONS

APPENDIX:
TECHNICAL DETAILS

SUMMARY

The summary should be an 'elevator pitch' (see Section 7.2) that captures the business issues, how the proposal addresses them and why your company is uniquely positioned to partner with the client. If your company is the current supplier, explain why any new ideas in the proposal haven't already been suggested.

BUSINESS CONTEXT AND CHALLENGES

These should reflect the brief, but restating the challenge more clearly or adding relevant context will help make your proposal more impressive. This is your chance to demonstrate that you understand your client's world, the challenges they face and the pressures they're under.

ADDRESSING THE CHALLENGES

Explain how your company is equipped to meet each challenge, describing features that deliver advantages to the client and emphasizing any that competitors cannot match. Bring to life what the client will receive via demonstrations or mock-ups.

OVERVIEW OF PROPOSED SOLUTION

Describe exactly what you propose to do to meet the client's needs. If the solution is particularly complex, summarize the purpose of each component and how they fit together.

TEAM AND SERVICING

Identify key members of the team by name, stating their roles and relevant credentials. This makes your proposal more credible and personal.

FUTURE PROOFING

For ongoing assignments, describe how working with you would allow the client to access and benefit from the latest ideas, methods and technologies. Even if not explicitly requested in the brief, refer to any innovative approaches in development that they could benefit from in future.

INVESTMENT OPTIONS

For complex projects, providing two or three options may be helpful. If you know the client's project budget, your recommended option should be priced just below it (and expect subsequent negotiations to bring the price down 5–10%). If you don't know the budget, make an estimate and provide options with prices significantly below, equal to and significantly above your estimate to increase the chances of one option falling into the right zone. Explain the benefits and trade-offs of each option, but make each sound attractive in its own right.

Some companies define a set of criteria against which to assess bids. If the client has revealed these, include a summary explaining how each criterion is met by different elements of your proposal. If the criteria have not been disclosed, use the following as a guide:
- Understanding of the business and its challenges
- Sector expertise
- Relevance and validity of solution proposed
- Quality of servicing
- Ability to cope with the scale of the project, and deliver subsequent reliability
- Innovative thinking/continual improvement

Make it easy for people assessing your proposal to find reasons to score it well across the board. Getting a big tick against all criteria won't guarantee that you'll win the business, but it should put you among the strongest contenders.

10.4 MAKING IT PERSONAL

When choosing a business partner, people use their gut feel at least as much as logical thinking. They prefer to award business to a team they like and believe they'd enjoy working with. Conversely, they'll never sign a deal with anyone they mistrust. When pitching for new business, how you make the client feel at every stage of the process will affect how they rate your proposal and drive their final decision. In addition to building rapport and trust (see Section 6.3), here are some things you can do to tip the balance in your favour.

PROVIDING THE PERSONAL TOUCH

CHOOSE A TEAM THE CLIENT WILL LOVE

SHOW THE CLIENT YOU REALLY WANT TO PARTNER THEM

EXPLAIN OFFER IN TERMS OF BENEFITS TO THEM

NEED
⇧
BENEFIT
⇧
FEATURE

PROVIDE A TASTE OF THE PERSONAL ATTENTION YOU OFFER

Based on what you told us, we think we could help you with XXX - our thoughts on this are attached.

Is there anything more we could provide that would help you with your decision?

We've noticed a lot of interest in XXX in your business, so we thought the attached article might be useful.

What could we provide to help you bring your boss/colleagues around to your way of thinking?

Choosing the right team is vital. If someone in your business already has a strong relationship with the client, they should be part of the pitch team. Everyone else involved should be chosen in the belief that the client will get on well with them too. It's also worth preparing something to show the client how much the team wants to work with them. This could be a short video of team members expressing their excitement about the project, or a message from your CEO saying how much they'd value the client's business. How you interact with clients during the process gives them an idea of what it would be like to work with you. And so, it's important to be as attentive, thoughtful and as proactive as possible.

Before they can choose a partner, the decision-makers need to feel confident that the appointment would be accepted by the wider business. A clash of corporate values or individual personalities might impair collaboration, so it pays to make the company and the team look, feel and sound like they'll fit in well. Here are some ideas on how to do this.

MAKE IT FEEL LIKE THEIRS

REFLECT THEIR VALUES & TONE OF VOICE

Show how well the values of the two organizations align.

USE A DESIGN STYLE THAT MATCHES THEIRS

But make sure your logo is also prominent.

AVOID USING ACRONYMS, ABBREVIATIONS & JARGON

Only use technical terms you are sure everyone understands.

ADOPT THEIR FRAMEWORKS & TERMINOLOGY

If you want to recommend your own, show how well it fits their thinking and explain the benefits of adopting yours.

ILLUSTRATE DELIVERABLES AS THEY'D APPEAR IN THEIR COMPANY

Wherever possible, illusrate deliverables using their data, brands, relationships, etc. rather than generic sales examples.

10.5 ENGAGING PITCH PRESENTATIONS

Pitches are similar to other presentations, but the stakes are higher, and you usually have to do more to prove your credentials. The outcome could determine the fortunes of your business, so you'll need to prepare more thoroughly and pay attention to all the details, starting with casting.

When choosing your presentation team, aim to:
- Involve the right number of people; avoid outnumbering client attendees
- Include the key people who would work on the business
- Prioritize those whom the client already trusts, and others they're likely to connect with
- Pick people who add credibility to the main points you need to land — if operational excellence is important, include the operations expert
- Have separate presenters personify each of the top priorities — with each making a personal commitment to the client — to enhance credibility, emphasize the sense of personal ownership and make it easy for the audience to remember your key points

PERSONAL PLEDGES

When it comes to delivering the pitch, prepare thoroughly and allow plenty of time to make the presentation engaging. Chapter 8 explains how to do this, but here are the aspects of presenting that are especially important in new business pitches because of the need to engage and impress the audience:

TIPS FOR AN ENGAGING PITCH

REHEARSE THOROUGHLY

Practise as a team and give each other suggestions on making the presentation stronger, allowing time for individuals to re-prepare privately before the next rehearsal. If your rehearsals last longer than the time allotted for the client meeting, edit-down the content. And always have a plan for what to skip on the fly, if there's a chance you might run over.

BREAK THE ICE

At the start of a new business pitch, people tend to be more nervous than in other types of presentations, so try to break the ice with a humorous observation or an anecdote connecting you with the client company. Try to foster a relaxed, positive atmosphere and let your personality come through, which will help diffuse any tensions.

RE-ENERGIZE EVERY 20 MINUTES

Plan to include regular audience participation, to maintain high levels of attention. Use variety to keep the audience awake and engaged. Find ways to illustrate ideas in a lively, engaging manner.

SHOW DEMOS AND MOCK-UPS

These help clients understand the deliverables and introduce variety to the delivery. If using a live demo, always prepare an alternate way of presenting the same content — like having a complete set of backup screenshots ready to go — in case the technology lets you down.

USING QUESTIONS

In pitch presentations, asking questions serves two purposes: they help engage the audience and can help gauge whether if the ideas you've presented are resonating. If you feel that audience members aren't convinced about some element, say something like, 'I'm sensing that you're unsure. What are your thoughts on this?'

HAVE AN UPLIFTING FINISH

The feeling people are left with at the end of an experience is known to have the biggest influence on their overall impression of it. For example, even a movie that's been consistently compelling is remembered as a negative experience if the ending is disappointing. This is why you need an uplifting finish for your pitch.

Aim to leave the audience with an inspiring idea that reinforces why working with you would be uniquely beneficial to them. In the end, you and your audience should walk away convinced that it's been a constructive, win-win experience for everyone involved.

Speaking of uplifting finishes, you have now reached the end of *The Soft Skills Book.*

The hope is that you will come away with an understanding of the wide range of soft skills at your disposal, and a good deal of the valuable general business knowledge, that taken together can help you enjoy a thriving, successful career.

Soft skills are often underestimated, yet they can be the key differentiator that helps you become truly effective and be seen as a valued member of a team or company. They unleash the power of your personality, attitude, motivation, and social and emotional intelligence.

As the author said in the introduction, every job requires different strengths and capabilities, but soft skills form the backbone of any successful career.

The pitch to you is simple: if you can apply half of what's been covered in this book, while developing the technical know-how needed in your field, you'll set yourself apart from most other business professionals.

The author hopes you enjoy the ride, and wishes you the best of luck in all your endeavours.

ABOUT THE AUTHOR

DAN WHITE is a business innovator. His ideas about the science of marketing, and the art of succeeding within business, have influenced generations of young professionals.

In his early career, Dan learnt how to build client relationships and successful teams. He went on the become Chief Marketing Officer for the well-known marketing research company Millward Brown, where for over twenty years he has been responsible for product development, marketing and internal communications across Europe, Middle East and Africa.

Dan then turned his attention to capability development as Head of Expertise for Kantar's insights division in the UK. In this role he created a blueprint for professional development, identifying what someone within a professional service company needs to learn in order to succeed and the best way for them to gain the necessary skills and knowledge over the course of their career.

This insight has been distilled into the ideas and unique visualizations presented in *The Soft Skills Book*.

FROM THE SAME AUTHOR

The Smart Marketing Book
LID Publishing, 2020

FURTHER PRAISE FOR
THE SOFT SKILLS BOOK

"This little treasure of a book breaks down all the soft skills that every professional needs in order to succeed. The complex is made super crisp and simple with practical ideas and engaging visuals. Want to be better at presenting, pitching, storytelling, team leading, project management, networking, workshopping and so much more? It is all there!"

Barbara Cador, Vice President, Growth Officer Europe at Behaviorally

"*The Soft Skills Book* is solid gold. So many actionable tips and tricks for everyday business situations. I've recommended it to all my colleagues."

Dr. Sebastian Wolf, Unit Creative Director & interim Head of Strategy at TERRITORY

"A reference library of well explained ideas that can help anyone develop the skills that make them, and their business, work better."

Marc Binkley, Vice President for Digital & Marketing Strategy at Anstice Communications

"A really nice, succinct snapshot of soft skills put forward in an authentic tone of voice and with the right balance of ideas and practical advice. It's like a compass to guide you through those everyday work experiences to not only be more successful in your work, but to be left feeling more efficient, effective and fulfilled in what you do. I can see this becoming a sort of Bible of Everyday Work."

AJ Rollsy, Founder at HealthPoint Research